ACETARIA.

A

DISCOURSE

OF

SALLETS.

By *J. E.* S. R. S. Author of
the *Kalendarium.*

Οὐ παντὸς ανδρὸς ἐστιν ἀρτῦσαι καλῶς.
Crat. in Glauc.

LONDON,

Printed for *B. Tooke* at the *Middle-Temple* Gate in *Fleetstreet*, 1699.

COPY NUMBER
200

This facsimile edition published in 1982
by Prospect Books,
45 Lamont Road, London SW10 0HU

Design consultant Dave Grogan

Printed by Latimer Trend & Company Ltd,
Crescent Avenue, Plymouth PL1 3AW

Bound by Robert Hartnoll, Bodmin

ISBN 0 9073 2512 2

TO THE

Right Honourable

J O H N
Lord SO MERS
O F
E V E S H A M.

Lord *High - Chancellor* of
England, and *President* of
the *Royal-Society.*

My Lord,

THE *Idea* and *Plan* of
the *Royal-Society,* ha‧
ving been first con‧
ceiv'd and delineated by a
A   *Great*

Great and *Learned Chancellor*, which High Office your Lordſhip deſervedly bears ; not as an Acquiſition of Fortune, but your Intellectual Endowments ; Conſpicuous (among other Excellencies) by the Inclination Your Lordſhip diſcovers to promote *Natural Knowledge* :   As it juſtifies the Diſcernment of that *Aſſembly*, to pitch upon Your Lordſhip for their *Preſident*, ſo does it no leſs diſcover the Candor, yea, I preſume to ſay, the Sublimity of your Mind, in ſo generouſly honoring them with your *Acceptance* of the *Choice* they have made.

A

The Dedication.

A *Chancellor*, and a very Learned Lord, was the *First* who honoured the *Chair*; and a no lefs Honorable and Learned *Chancellor*, refigns it to Your Lordſhip: So as after all the Difficulties and Hardſhips the *Society* has hitherto gone through; it has thro' the Favour and Protection of its *Prefidents*, not only preferv'd its Reputation from the Malevolence of Enemies and Detracters, but gone on *Culminating*, and now *Triumphantly* in Your Lordſhip: Under whofe propitious Influence, I am perſwaded, it may promife it ſelf *That*, which indeed has

A 2 　　　　　hi-

Lord Vifcount Brouncker, Chancellor to the Late Qu. Confort, now Dowager. The Right Honourable Cha. Montague, Efq; Chancellor of the Exchequer.

hitherto been wanting, to justifie the Glorious *Title* it bears of a ROYAL SOCIE-TY. The *Emancipating* it from some Remaining and Discouraging Circumstances, which it as yet labours under; among which, that of a *Precarious* and unsteady Abode, is not the least.

This *Honor* was reserv'd for Your Lordship; and an *Honor*, permit me to call it, not at all unworthy the Owning of the Greatest Person living: Namely, the Establishing and Promoting *Real Knowledge*; and (next to what is *Divine*) truly so called; as far, at least, as Humane Nature

ture extends towards the Knowledge of Nature, by enlarging her Empire beyond the Land of *Spectres*, *Forms*, *Intentional Species*, *Vacuum*, *Occult Qualities*, and other *Inadæquate Notions*; which, by their Obstreperous and Noisy Disputes, affrighting, and (till of late) deterring Men from adventuring on further Discoveries, confin'd them in a lazy Acquiescence, and to be fed with *Fantasms* and fruitless Speculations, which signifie nothing to the *specifick* Nature of Things, solid and useful Knowledge; by the *Investigation* of *Causes*, *Principles*, *Energies*, *Powers*, and *Effects*

A 3

fects of *Bodies,* and *Things Visible;* and to improve them for the Good and Benefit of Mankind.

My Lord, That which the *Royal Society* needs to accomplish an entire Freedom, and (by rendring their Circumstances more easie) capable to subsist with Honor, and to reach indeed the Glorious Ends of its *Institution,* is an Establishment in a more Settl'd, *Appropriate,* and *Commodious Place;* having hitherto (like the *Tabernacle* in the *Wilderness*) been only *Ambulatory* for almost *Forty Years:* But *Solomon* built the First *Temple;* and what forbids us to hope, that

as

as *Great* a *Prince* may build *Solomon's House*, as that *Great Chancellor* (one of Your Lordship's Learned *Predecessors*) had design'd the *Plan*; there being nothing in that *August* and *Noble Model* impossible, or beyond the *Power* of *Naure* and Learned Industry.

Verulamii Atlantis

Thus, whilst King *Solomon's* Temple was *Consecrated* to the *God* of *Nature*, and his true Worship; *This* may be *Dedicated*, and set apart for the *Works* of *Nature*; deliver'd from those Illusions and Impostors, that are still endeavouring to cloud and depress the True, and *Substantial Philosophy*: A *shallow* and *Superficial Insight*,

A 4 wherein

wherein (as that Incomparable Perſon rightly obſerves) having made ſo many *Atheiſts*: whilſt a *profound*, and thorow *Penetration* into her *Receſſes* (which is the *Buſineſs* of the *Royal Society*) would lead Men to the *Knowledge*, and *Admiration* of the *Glorious Author*.

And now, *My Lord*, I expect ſome will wonder what my Meaning is, to uſher in a *Trifle*, with ſo much Magnificence, and end at laſt in a fine *Receipt* for the *Dreſſing* of a *Sallet* with an Handful of *Pot-Herbs*! But yet, *My Lord*, this *Subject*, as low and deſpicable as it appears, challenges a Part of *Natural Hiſtory*;

story ; and the Greateſt Princes have thought it no Diſ-
grace, not only to make it
their *Diverſion*, but their *Care*,
and to promote and encou-
rage it in the midſt of their
weightieſt Affairs: He who
wrote of the *Cedar* of *Libanus*,
wrote alſo of the *Hyſop which
grows upon the Wall.*

To verifie this, how much
might I ſay of *Gardens* and
Rural Employments, preferrable
to the Pomp and Grandeur of
other Secular Buſineſs , and
that in the Eſtimate of as
Great Men as any Age has
produc'd ! And it is of ſuch
Great Souls we have it record-
ed ; That after they had per-
form'd

form'd the Noblest Exploits
for thePublick,they sometimes
chang'd their *Scepters* for the
Spade, and their *Purple* for the
Gardiner's *Apron*. And of
these, some, *My Lord*, were
*Emperors, Kings, Consuls, Dicta-
tors*, and Wise *Statesmen*;
who amidst the most impor-
tant Affairs, both in Peace
and War, have quitted all
their Pomp and Dignity in
Exchange of this Learned
Pleasure : Nor that of the
most *refin'd* Part of *Agricul-
ture* (the *Philosophy* of the
Garden and *Parterre* only) but
of *Herbs*, and wholesome
Sallets, and other plain and
useful Parts of *Geoponicks*, and
Wrote

Wrote *Books* of *Tillage* and *Husbandry*; and took the *Plough-Tackle* for their *Banner*, and their *Names* from the *Grain* and *Pulse* they fow'd, as the Marks and Characters of the highest Honor.

But I proceed no farther on a *Topic* fo well known to Your Lordship: Nor urge I Examples of fuch Illuftrious Perfons laying afide their Grandeur, and even of deferting their Stations; (which would infinitely prejudice the Publick, when worthy Men are in Place, and at the Helm) But to fhew how confiftent the Diverfions of the *Garden* and *Villa* were, with

the

the higheſt and buſieſt Employment of the *Commonwealth*, and never thought a Reproch, or the leaſt Diminution to the Gravity and Veneration due to their Perſons, and the Noble Rank they held.

Will Your Lordſhip give me Leave to repeat what is ſaid of the Younger *Pliny*, (Nephew to the *Naturaliſt*) and whom I think we may parallel with the Greateſt of his time (and perhaps of any ſince) under the Worthieſt *Emperor* the *Roman* World ever had? A Perſon of vaſt Abilities, Rich, and High in his Maſter's Favour; that

ſo

ſo Husbanded his time, as in the Midſt of the weightieſt Affairs, to have Anſwer'd, and by his ✱ *Example*, made good what I have ſaid on this Occaſion. The Ancient and beſt Magiſtrates of *Rome*, allow'd but the *Ninth* Day for the *City* and *Publick Buſineſs*; the reſt for the *Country* and the *Sallet Garden*: There were then fewer *Cauſes* indeed

---

✱ *Si quid temporis à civilibus negotiis, quibus totum jam intenderat animum, ſuffurari potuit, colendis agris, priſcos illos* Romanos *Numam Pompilium, Cincinnatum, Catonem, Fabios, Cicerones, alioſque virtute claros viros imitare*; *qui in magno honore conſtituti, vites putare, ſtercorare agros, & irrigare nequaquam turpe & inhoneſtum putarunt.* In Vit. Plin. 2.

at

at the *Bar* ; but never greater *Justice*, nor better *Judges* and *Advocates*. And 'tis hence observed, that we hardly find a Great and Wise Man among the Ancients, *qui nullos habuit hortos*, excepting only *Pomponius Atticus* ; whilst his Dear *Cicero* professes, that he never laid out his Money more readily, than in the purchasing of *Gardens*, and those sweet Retirements, for which he so often left the *Rostra* (and Court of the Greatest and most flourishing State of the World) to visit, prune, and water them with his own Hands.

But,

But, *My Lord,* I forget with whom I am talking thus; and a *Gardiner* ought not to be so bold. The Present I humbly make Your Lordship, is indeed but a *Sallet* of *Crude Herbs* : But there is among them that which was a *Prize* at the *Isthmian Games* ; and Your Lordship knows who it was both accepted, and rewarded as despicable an Oblation of this kind. The Favor I humbly beg, is Your Lordship's Pardon for this Presumption. The Subject is *mean,* and requires it, and my *Reputation* in danger ; should Your Lordship hence suspect that one could never write so much

much of *dressing Sallets*, who minded any thing serious, besides the gratifying a Sensual Appetite with a Voluptuary *Apician* Art.

Truly, *My Lord*, I am so far from designing to promote those *Supplicia Luxuriæ*, (as *Seneca* calls them) by what I have here written; that were it in my Power, I would recall the World, if not altogether to their Pristine *Diet*, yet to a much more *wholsome* and *temperate* than is now in Fashion: And what if they find me like to some who are eager after *Hunting* and other Field Sports, which are *Laborious* Exercises? and *Fishing*, which

which is indeed a *Lazy* one ? who, after all their Pains and Fatigue, never eat what they take and catch in either : For some such I have known : And tho' I cannot affirm so of my self, (when a well drest and excellent *Sallet* is before me) I am yet a very moderate Eater of them. So as to this *Book-Luxury*, I can affirm, and that truly what the *Poet* says of himself (on a less innocent Occasion) *Lasciva pagina, vita proba.* God forbid, that after all I have advanc'd in Praise of *Sallets*, I should be thought to plead for the Vice I censure, and chuse that of *Epicurus* for

a   my

my *Lemma*; *In hac arte con-
senui* ; or to have ſpent my
time in nothing elſe. The *Plan*
annext to theſe Papers, and
the *Apparatus* made to ſuper-
ſtruct upon it, would acquit
me of having bent all my
Contemplations on *Sallets* only. What I humbly offer
Your Lordſhip, is (as I ſaid)
Part of *Natural Hiſtory*, the
Product of *Horticulture* , and
the *Field*, dignified by the moſt
illuſtrious, and ſometimes til-
led *Laureato Vomere* ; which, as it
concerns a Part of *Philoſophy*, I
may (without Vanity) be allow'd to have taken ſome
Pains in Cultivating, as an inferior Member of the *Royal
Society.*   But,

But, *My Lord*, whilst You read on (if at least You vouchsafe me that Honor to read at all) I am conscious I rob the Publick of its most Precious Moments.

I therefore Humbly again Implore Your Lordship's Pardon : Nor indeed needed I to have said half this, to kindle in Your Breast , that which is already shining there (Your Lordship's Esteem of the *Royal Society*) after what You were pleas'd to Express in such an Obliging manner , when it was lately to wait

a 2　　　upon

upon Your Lordſhip; a-
mong whom I had the Ho-
nor to be a Witneſs of
Your Generous, and Favourable Acceptance of their Ad-
dreſſes, who am,

My Lord,

Your Lordſhip's

Moſt Humble and

Moſt Obedient Servant,

JOHN EVELYN.

THE

THE

PREFACE.

THE Favourable Entertainment which the Kalendar has found, encouraging the Bookseller to adventure upon a Ninth Impression, I could not refuse his Request of my Revising, and Giving it the best Improvement I was capable, to an Inexhaustible Subject, as it regards a Part of Horticulture ; and offer some little Aid to such as love a Diversion so Innocent and Laudable. There are those of late, who have

a 3 arro.

arrogated, *and given the Glorious Title of* Compleat *and* Accomplish'd Gardiners, *to what they have* Publish'd; *as if there were nothing wanting, nothing more remaining, or farther to be expected from the Field; and that* Nature *had been quite emptied of all her fertile Store:* Whilst *those who thus magnifie their Discoveries, have after all, penetrated but a very little Way into this* Vast, Ample, *and as yet,* Unknown Territory; *Who see not, that it would still require the* Revolution *of many* Ages; *deep, and long* Experience, *for any Man to* Emerge *that* Perfect, *and* Accomplish'd Artist Gardiner *they boast themselves to be:* Nor do I think

think, Men will ever reach the End, and far extended Limits of the Vegetable Kingdom, *so incomprehensible is the Variety it every Day produces, of the most Useful, and Admirable of all the Aspectable Works of God; since almost all we see, and touch, and taste, and smell, eat and drink, are clad with, and defended (from the Greatest Prince to the Meanest Peasant) is furnished from that Great and Universal Plantation, Epitomiz d in our Gardens, highly worth the Contemplation of the most Profonnd Divine, and Deepest Philosopher.*

The Preface.

I should be asham'd to acknowledge how little I have advanc'd, could I find that ever any Mortal Man from Adam, Noah, Solomon, Aristotle, Theophrastus, Dioscorides, *and the rest of Nature's Interpreters, had ever arriv'd to the perfect Knowledge of any one* Plant, *or* Vulgar Weed *whatsoever :* But this perhaps may yet possibly be reserv'd for another State of Things, and a * longer Day ; that is, When Time shall be no more, but Knowledge shall be encreas'd.

---

* Ut hujusmodi historiam vix dum incohatum, non ante absolvendam putem,

Exitio terras quam dabit una dies. *D. Raius* Præfat. Hist. Plan.

We

The Preface.

We have heard of one who studied and contemplated the Nature of Bees only, for Sixty Years : *After which, you will not wonder, that a Person of my Acquaintance, should have spent almost* Forty, *in Gathering and Amassing Materials for an* Hortulan Design, *to so enormous an Heap, as to fill some* Thousand Pages ; *and yet be comprehended within two, or three Acres of Ground ; nay, within the Square of less than* One *(skilfully Planted and Cultivated) sufficient to furnish, and entertain his Time and Thoughts all his Life long, with a most Innocent, Agreeable, and Useful Employment. But you may justly won-*

der,

The Preface.

der, and *Condemn the Vanity of it too, with that Reproach,* This

Luke 15. 30.

Man began to build, but was not able to finish! *This has been the Fate of that Undertaking ; and I dare promise, will be of whosoever imagines (without the Circumstances of extraordinary Assistance, and no ordinary Expence) to pursue the Plan, erect, and finish the Fabrick as it ought to be.*

But this is that which Abortives the Perfection of the most Glorious and Useful Undertakings; the Unsatiable Coveting to Exhaust all that should, or can be said upon every Head : If such a one have any thing else to mind, or do in the World, let me tell him, he thinks of

build-

The Preface.

Building too late ; and rarely find we any, who care to superstruct upon the Foundation of another, and whose Ideas are alike. There ought therefore to be as many Hands, *and Subsidiaries to such a Design (and those* Masters *too) as there are distinct Parts of the Whole (according to the subsequent Table) that those who have the* Means *and* Courage, *may (tho' they do not undertake the Whole) finish a Part at least, and in time Unite their Labours into one Intire, Compleat, and Consummate Work indeed.*

Of One or Two *of these, I attempted only a Specimen in my* SILVA *and the* KALENDAR;

The Preface.

DAR : *Imperfect, I say, because they are both capable of Great Improvements : It is not therefore to be expected. (Let me use the Words of an Old, and Experienc'd Gardiner)*

Columella *de* R. R. *Lib.* 5. *Cap.* 1. Cuncta me dicturum, quæ vastitas ejus scientiæ contineret, sed plurima ; nam illud in unius hominis prudentiam cadere non poterit , neque est ulla Disciplina aut Ars, quæ singulari consummata sit ingenio.

May it then suffice aliquam partem tradidisse, *and that I have done my Endeavour.*

----- Jurtilis olim Ne Videar vixisse.

Much

The Preface.

Much more might I add upon this Charming, and Fruitful Subject (I mean, concerning Gardening :) But this is not a Place to Expatiate, deterr'd, as I have long since been, from so bold an Enterprize, as the Fabrick I mentioned. I content my self then with an Humble Cottage *, and a* Simple Potagere, *Appendant to the* Calendar ; *which, Treating only (and that briefly) of the* Culture *of* Moderate Gardens ; *Nothing seems to me , shou'd be more* Welcome *and* Agreeable, *than whilst the Product of them is come into more Request and Use amongst us,*

than

than heretofore (beside what
we call, and distinguish by
the Name of Fruit) I did an-
nex some particular Directions concerning SALLETS.

THE

THE
PLAN
OF A
Royal Garden:

Deſcribing, and Shewing the *Amplitude*, and *Extent* of that Part of *Georgicks*, which belongs to *Horticulture*;

In Three Books.

BOOK I.

Chap. I. **O**F *Principles* and *Elements* in general.

Ch. II. Of the Four (vulgarly reputed) Elements; *Fire, Air, Water, Earth.*

Ch. III.

BOOK II.

Ch.

Ch.

Ch.

The Plan of a

―――*Laudato ingentia rura,*
　　Exiguum colito.―――

ERRATA.

Page.	Line.	Read	Page.	Line.	Read
Title,	o 6	ἐϛιν.			
Dedicat.	7 8	*Nature*	50	12	*resiſt*
Præface,	8 penult.	*inutilis*	62	15	*Potagere*
Plan, Book 3 cap. 4.		*Gum*	74	7	*dele not*
		(*Commeſſa*	9o	5	*llanders*
Acetar.	5 10	*dele accept*	123	14	ἐϛιν
	6 17	*of which*	125	17	*Cataclyſm*
	16 8	*Halmyridia*	158	Marg.	*Eſu ſan-*
	18 20	*are eaten*			(*guinis*
	26 24	*Sage*	162	13	*dele and*
	33 11	*Oxelæum*	166	18	*Friers*
	34 4	*Coſſ Lettuce*	183	20	*a well-ſtor'd*
	42 16	*Pig-Nuts*	186	Mult.	*Skirrits*
	48 14	*dele Clove,*	189	19	*Meaths,*
		read Seeds.			

In the APPENDIX,

RECEITS.

Number 14. *Cucumber. Note,* That the *Cucumbers* and the *Gerkems* are not to be boiled in either of the *Vinegars*; but poured ſcalding-hot upon them.——And line 7, r. *next day, or longer.*

26. *Pudding* of *Carrots. Read thus :* Pare of the Cruſt and tougher part of a Two-peny White-Loaf, grating the reſt; as alſo half as much of the Root, a Pint of freſh Cream, or &c.

In the *Cowſlip-Wine* dele *two*; read *ten Gallons,*

ACETARIA.

SALLETS in general consist of certain *Esculent* Plants and Herbs, improv'd by Culture, Industry, and Art of the *Gard'ner :* Or, as others say, they are a Composition of *Edule* Plants and Roots of several kinds, to be eaten *Raw* or *Green*, *Blanch'd* or *Candied* ; simple, and *per se*, or intermingl'd with others according to the Season. The Boil'd, Bak'd, Pickl'd, or otherwise disguis'd, variously accommodated by the skilful Cooks, to render them grateful to the more feminine Palat, or Herbs rather for the Pot, *&c.* challenge not the name of *Sallet* so properly

B   here,

here, tho' sometimes mention'd;
And therefore,

Those who *Criticize* not so
nicely upon the Word, seem to
distinguish the * *Olera* (which
were never eaten *Raw*) from
Acetaria, which were never
Boil'd; and so they derive the
Etymology of *Olus*, from *Olla*,
the Pot. But others deduce
it from Ὅλος, comprehending
the *Universal Genus* of the Vegetable Kingdom; as from Πᾶν
Panis; esteeming that he who
had || *Bread* and *Herbs*, was suf-
ficiently bless'd with all a frugal
Man cou'd need or desire: O-

---

* Olera à frigidis distinct. *See* Spartianus in
Pescennio. Salmas. in Jul. Capitolin.
|| Panis erat primis virides mortalibus Herbæ;
    Quas tellus nullo sollicitante dabat.
Et modo carpebant vivaci cespite gramen;
    Nunc epulæ tenera fronde cacumen erant.
Ovid, Fastor. iv.

thers

thers again will have it, *ab Olendo,* i. e. *Crescendo,* from its continual *growth* and *springing up* : So the younger *Scaliger* on *Varro* : But his Father *Julius* extends it not so generally to all *Plants,* as to all the *Esculents,* according to the Text : *We call those* Olera (says * *Theophrastus*) *which are commonly eaten,* in which sense it may be taken, to include both *Boil'd* and *Raw* : Last of all, *ab Alendo,* as having been the Original, and genuine Food of all Mankind from the † Creation.

A great deal more of this Learned Stuff were to be pick'd up from the *Cumini Sectores,* and impertinently Curious; whilst as it concerns the business in hand, we are by *Sallet* to understand

---

* καλῦμεν γὰς λάχανα τὰ πρὸς τὴν ἡμετέραν χρείαν, Theophrast. Plant. *l.* vii. *cap.*7. † Gen. 1. 29.

a particular Compofition of
certain *Crude* and frefh Herbs,
fuch as ufually are, or may
fafely be eaten with fome *A-
cetous* Juice, *Oyl*, *Salt*, &c. to
give them a grateful Guft and
Vehicle; exclufive of the * ψυχραὶ
τράπεζαι, eaten without their
due Correctives, which the Learned † *Salmafius*, and, indeed generally, the ‖ old *Phyſicians* affirm (and that truly) all *Crude*
and raw λάχανα require to render them wholfome; fo as probably they were from hence,
as ¶ *Pliny* thinks, call'd *Acetaria:*
and not (as *Hermolaus* and fome
others) *Acceptaria ab Accipiendo*;
nor from *Accedere*, though fo

---

* Plutarch Sympof.
† Salmaf. in Solin. *againſt* Hieron. Mer-
curialis.
‖ Galen. 2 R. Aliment. *cap.* 1. Et Simp.
Medic. Averroes, *lib.* v. Colloc.
¶ Plin. *lib.* xix. *c.* 4.

* ready

* ready at hand, and easily
dress'd; requiring neither *Fire,
Cost*, or *Attendance*, to boil, roast,
and prepare them as did Flesh,
and other Provisions; from
which, and other Prerogatives,
they were always in use, *&c.*
And hence indeed the more
frugal *Italians* and *French*, to this
Day, Accept and gather *Ogni
Verdura*, any thing almost that's
Green and Tender, to the very
Tops of *Nettles*; so as every
Hedge affords a *Sallet* (not una-
greeable) season'd with its proper *Oxybaphon* of *Vinegar, Salt,
Oyl,* &c. which doubtless gives
it both the Relish and Name of
Salad, Ensalada †, as with us of
Sallet; from the *Sapidity*, which
renders not *Plants* and *Herbs*

---

* Convictus facilis, sine arte mensa.
Mart. Ep. 74.

† Ἀπυρον τροφήν, *which* Suidas *calls*
λάχανα, Olera quæ cruda sumuntur ex
Aceto. *Harduin in loc.*

alone,

alone, but *Men* themselves, and their Conversations, pleasant and agreeable : But of this enough, and perhaps too much ; least whilst I write of *Salt* and *Sallet*, I appear my self *Insipid:* I pass therefore to the Ingredients, which we will call

Furniture *and* Materials.

THE *Materials* of *Sallets,* which together with the grosser *Olera,* consist of *Roots, Stalks, Leaves, Buds, Flowers,* &c. *Fruits (* belonging to another *Class)* would require a much ampler Volume, than would suit our *Kalendar,* (to which this pretends to be an *Appendix* only) should we extend the following *Catalogue* further than to a brief enumeration only of such *Herbaceous*

baceous Plants, *Oluscula* and smaller *Esculents*, as are chiefly us'd in *Cold Sallets*, of whose Culture we have treated there; and as we gather them from the *Mother* and *Genial Bed*, with a touch only of their *Qualities*, for Reasons hereafter given.

1. Alexanders, *Hipposelinum*; *S. Smyrnium vulgare* (much of the nature of *Persly*) is moderately hot, and of a cleansing Faculty, Deobstructing, nourishing, and comforting the Stomach. The gentle fresh Sprouts, Buds, and Tops are to be chosen, and the Stalks eaten in the Spring; and when *Blanch'd*, in Winter likewise, with *Oyl, Peper, Salt,* &c. by themselves, or in Composition: They make also an excellent *Vernal* Pottage.

2. Artichaux, *Cinara*, (*Cardus Sativus*) hot and dry. The
Heads

Heads being flit in quarters firft
eaten raw, with *Oyl*, a little
Vinegar, *Salt*, and *Pepper*, grate-
fully recommend a Glafs of *Wine*;
Dr *Muffet* fays, at the end of
Meals.

They are likewife, whilft tender and fmall, fried in frefh
Butter crifp with *Persley*. But
then become a moft delicate and
excellent Reftorative, when full
grown, they are boil'd the common way. The *Bottoms* are alfo
bak'd in *Pies*, with *Marrow*,
Dates, and other rich Ingredients : In *Italy* they fometimes
broil them, and as the Scaly
Leaves open, bafte them with
frefh and fweet *Oyl*; but with
Care extraordinary, for if a drop
fall upon the Coals, all is marr'd;
that hazard efcap'd, they eat
them with the Juice of *Orange*
and *Sugar*.

The Stalk is *Blanch*'d in Autumn, and the *Pith* eaten raw

or

or boil'd. The way of pre-
ferving them frefh all Winter,
is by feparating the *Bottoms*
from the *Leaves*, and after Par-
boiling, allowing to every *Bottom*, a fmall earthen glaz'd Pot;
burying it all over in frefh melted
Butter, as they do Wild-Fowl,
&c. Or if more than one, in a
larger Pot, in the fame Bed and
Covering, *Layer* upon *Layer*.

They are alfo preferv'd by
ftringing them on Pack-thread,
a clean Paper being put between every *Bottom*, to hinder
them from touching one another,
and fo hung up in a dry place.
They are likewife *Pickl'd.*

Tis not very long fince this
noble *Thiftle* came firft into *Italy*,
Improv'd to this Magnitude by
Culture; and fo rare in *England*,
that they were commonly fold
for *Crowns* a piece: But what
Carthage yearly fpent in them
(as *Pliny* computes the Sum)
amounted

amounted to *Sestertia Sena Millia*, 30000 *l. Sterling.*

Note, That the *Spanish Cardon*, a wild and smaller *Artichoak*, with sharp pointed Leaves, and lesser Head; the Stalks being *Blanch*'d and tender, are serv'd-up *a la Poiverade* (that is with *Oyl*, *Pepper*, &c.) as the *French* term is.

3. Basil, *Ocimum* (as *Baulm*) imparts a grateful Flavour, if not too strong, somewhat offensive to the Eyes; and therefore the tender Tops to be very sparingly us'd in our *Sallet*.

4. Baulm, *Melissa*, *Baum*, hot and dry, Cordial and exhilarating, sovereign for the Brain, strengthning the Memory, and powerfully chasing away *Melancholy*. The tender Leaves are us'd in Composition with other Herbs; and the Sprigs fresh gather'd,

ther'd, put into *Wine* or other
Drinks, during the heat of Summer, give it a marvellous quickness : This noble Plant yields an
incomparable *Wine*, made as is
that of *Cowslip*-Flowers.

5. Beet, *Beta* ; of which
there is both *Red*, *Black*, and
White : The *Costa*, or Rib of the
White Beet (by the *French* call'd
the *Chard*) being boil'd, melts,
and eats like Marrow. And the
Roots (especially of the *Red*)
cut into thin slices, boil'd, when
cold, is of it self a grateful Winter *Sallet* ; or being mingl'd with
other *Oluscula*, *Oyl*, *Vinegar*, *Salt*,
&c. 'Tis of quality Cold and
Moist, and naturally somewhat
Laxative : But however by the
Epigrammatist stil'd *Foolish* and
Insipid, as *Innocentior quam Olus*
(for so the Learned * *Harduin*

---

* Plin. H. Nat. *lib.* xix. *cap.* 8.

reads

reads the place) 'tis by *Diphilus* of old, and others since, preferr'd before *Cabbage* as of better Nourishment: *Martial* (not unlearn'd in the Art of *Sallet*) commends it with *Wine* and *Pepper:* He names it indeed —— *Fabrorum prandia,* for its being so vulgar. But eaten with *Oyl* and *Vinegar,* as usually, it is no despicable *Sallet.* There is a *Beet* growing near the Sea, which is the most delicate of all. The Roots of the *Red Beet,* pared into thin Slices and Circles, are by the *French* and *Italians* contriv'd into curious Figures to adorn their *Sallets.*

6. Blite, *Blitum*; English *Mercury,* or (as our Country House-wives call it) *All-good,* the gentle *Turiones,* and Tops may be eaten as *Sparagus,* or sodden in Pottage: There is both a white and red, much us'd in *Spain* and *Italy*; but besides its humidity and

and deterſive Nature, 'tis *Inſipid* enough.

7. Borrage, *Borrago (Gaudia ſemper ago)* hot and kindly moiſt, purifying the Blood, is an exhilarating Cordial, of a pleaſant Flavour : The tender Leaves, and Flowers eſpecially, may be eaten in Compoſition ; but above all, the Sprigs in *Wine*, like thoſe of *Baum*, are of known Vertue to revive the *Hypochondriac*, and chear the hard Student. See *Bugloſs*.

8. Brooklime, *Anagallis aquatica* ; moderately hot and moiſt, prevalent in the *Scorbute*, and *Stone*.

9. Bugloſs, *Bugloſſum* ; in nature much like *Borrage*, yet ſomething more aſtringent. The Flowers of both, with the intire Plant, greatly reſtorative, being Con-

Conserv'd: And for the reſt, ſo much commended by *Averroes*; that for its effects, cheriſhing the Spirits, juſtly call'd *Euphroſynum:* Nay, ſome will have it the *Ne-penthes* of *Homer:* But indeed, what we now call *Bugloſs*, was not that of the Ancients, but ra-ther *Borrage*, for the like Virtue named *Corrago*.

Burnet, See *Pimpinella*.

10 Buds, *Gemmæ*, *Turiones*; the firſt Rudiments and Tops of moſt *Sallet*-Plants, preferrable to all other leſs tender Parts; ſuch as *Aſhen-Keys*, *Broom-buds*, hot and dry, retaining the vertue of *Capers*, eſteem'd to be very open-ing, and prevalent againſt the *Spleen* and *Scurvy*; and being *Pickl'd*, are ſprinkl'd among the *Sallets*, or eaten by themſelves.

11. Cab-

11. Cabbage, *Brassica* (and its several kinds) *Pompey's* beloved Dish, so highly celebrated by old * *Cato*, *Pythagoras*, and *Chrysippus* the Physician (as the only *Panacea*) is not so generally magnify'd by the rest of Doctors, as affording but a crass and melancholy Juice ; yet *Loosening* if but moderately boil'd, if over - much, *Astringent*, according to *C. Celsus* ; and therefore seldom eaten raw, excepting by the *Dutch*. The *Cymæ*, or Sprouts rather of the *Cole* are very delicate, so boil'd as to retain their Verdure and green Colour. In raising this *Plant* great care is to be had of the Seed. The best comes from *Denmark* and *Russia*, especially the *Cauly-flower*, (anciently unknown) or from *Aleppo*. Of the *French*, the *Pancaliere a la large*

---

* *De R. R. cap.* clvii.

Costé,

Costé, the white, large and pon-
derous are to be chosen; and so
the *Cauly-flower* : After boiling
some steep them in Milk, and
seethe them again in Beef-Broth :
Of old they added a little *Nitre*.
The *Broccoli* from *Naples*, perhaps the *Halmerida* of *Pliny* (or
Athenæus rather) *Capitata marina*
& *florida*, our *Sea-keele* (the ancient *Crambe*) and growing on
our Coast, are very delicate, as
are the *Savoys*, commended for
being not so rank, but agreeable
to most *Palates*, and of better
Nourishment : In general, *Cabbages* are thought to allay Fumes,
and prevent Intoxication : But
some will have them noxious to
the Sight ; others impute it to
the *Cauly-flower* rather : But whilst
the Learned are not agreed about
it, *Theophrastus* affirms the contrary, and *Pliny* commends the
Juice raw, with a little *Honey*,
for the moist and weeping Eye,
not

not the dry or dull. But after all, *Cabbage* ('tis confess'd) is greatly accus'd for lying undi- gested in the Stomach, and pro- voking Eructations; which makes me wonder at the Veneration we read the Ancients had for them, calling them *Divine*, and Swearing, *per Brassicam.* 'Tis scarce an hundred Years since we first had *Cabbages* out of *Holland.* Sir *Anth. Ashley* of *Wiburg St. Giles* in *Dorsetshire*, being (as I am told) the first who planted them in *England.*

12. Cardon, See *Artichaux.*

13. Carrots, *Dauci*, or *Pasti- naca Sativa*; temperately warm and dry, Spicy; the best are yellow, very nourishing; let them be rais'd in Ground natu- rally rich, but not too heavy.

C   14. Cher-

14. Chervile, *Chærophyllum*, *Myrrhis* ; The sweet aromatick *Spanish Chervile*, moderately hot and dry : The tender *Cimæ*, and Tops, with other Herbs, are never to be wanting in our *Sallets*, (as long as they may be had) being exceedingly wholsome and chearing the Spirits : The *Roots* are also boil'd and eaten Cold; much commended for Aged Persons : This (as likewise *Spinach*) is us'd in *Tarts*, and serves alone for divers Sauces.

Cibbols.⎱ *Vide* Onions, *Schæ-*
Cives. ⎰   *nopræsson.*

15. Clary, *Horminum*, when tender not to be rejected, and in *Omlets*, made up with *Cream*, fried in sweet *Butter*, and eaten with *Sugar*, Juice of *Orange*, or *Limon*.

16. Cla-

16. Clavers, *Aparine* ; the tender Winders, with young *Nettle-Tops*, are us'd in *Lenten* Pottages.

17. Corn-fallet, *Valerianella* ; loos'ning and refreshing : The Tops and Leaves are a *Sallet* of themfelves, feafonably eaten with other Salleting, the whole Winter long, and early Spring : The *French* call them *Salad de Preter*, for their being generally eaten in *Lent*.

18. Cowflips, *Paralyfis :* See *Flowers*.

19. Creffes, *Nafturtium*, Garden *Creffes* ; to be monthly fown : But above all the *Indian*, moderately hot, and aromatick, quicken the torpent Spirits, and purge the Brain, and are of fingular effect againft the *Scorbute*. Both the tender Leaves, *Calices*, Cappuchin

C 2

puchin Capers, and *Flowers*, are laudably mixed with the colder Plants. The *Buds* being Candy'd, are likewise us'd in Strewings all Winter. There is the *Naſtur. Hybernicum* commended alſo, and the vulgar *Water-Creſs*, proper in the Spring, all of the ſame Nature, tho' of different Degrees, and beſt for raw and cold Stomachs, but nouriſh little.

20. Cucumber, *Cucumis*; tho' very cold and moiſt, the moſt approved *Sallet* alone, or in Compoſition, of all the *Vinaigrets*, to ſharpen the Appetite, and cool the Liver, * &c. if rightly prepar'd; that is, by rectifying the vulgar Miſtake of altogether extracting the Juice, in which it ſhould rather be ſoak'd: Nor

---

* Ἐφ δὸς, δοσικυὸς, ἀπαλὸς, ἄλυαϲ⊙, ὑϛηππ̃- νὸς. Athen.

ought

ought it to be over *Oyl'd*, too
much abating of its grateful
Acidity, and *palling* the Taste,
from a contrariety of Particles :
Let them therefore be pared,
and cut in thin Slices, with a
Clove or two of *Onion* to correct
the Crudity, macerated in the
Juice, often turn'd and moderately drain'd. Others prepare
them, by shaking the Slices between two Dishes, and dress
them with very little *Oyl*, well
beaten, and mingled with the
Juice of *Limon, Orange,* or *Vinegar, Salt* and *Pepper.* Some a-
gain, (and indeed the most ap-
prov'd) eat them as soon as they
are cut, retaining their Liquor,
which being exhausted (by the
former Method) have nothing
remaining in them to help the
Concoction. Of old they * boil'd

---

* Cucumis elixus delicatior, innocentior.
Athenæus.

　　　　the

the *Cucumber*, and paring off the Rind, eat them with *Oyl*, *Vinegar*, and *Honey*; *Sugar* not being so well known. Lastly, the *Pulp* in Broth is greatly refreshing, and may be mingl'd in most *Sallets*, without the least damage, contrary to the common Opinion; it not being long, since *Cucumber*, however dress'd, was thought fit to be thrown away, being accounted little better than Poyson. *Tavernier* tells us, that in the *Levant*, if a Child cry for something to Eat, they give it a raw *Cucumber* instead of *Bread*. The young ones may be boil'd in White-Wine. The smaller sort (known by the name of *Gerckems*) muriated with the Seeds of *Dill*, and the *Mango* Pickle are for the Winter.

21. Daisy, *Buphthalmum*, Ox-Eye, or *Bellis-major:* The young *Roots* are frequently eaten by the
Spa-

Spaniards and *Italians* all the
Spring till *June.*

22. Dandelion, *Dens Leonis,*
Condrilla: Macerated in several
Waters, to extract the bitterness;
tho' somewhat opening, is very
wholsome, and little inferior to
Succory, Endive, &c. The *French*
Country-People eat the Roots;
and 'twas with this homely *Sallet,*
the Good-Wife *Hecate* entertain'd
Theseus. See *Sowthistle.*

23. Dock, *Oxylapathum,* or
sharp pointed Dock: Emollient,
and tho' otherwise not for our
Sallet, the *Roots* brewed in *Ale*
or *Beer,* are excellent for the
Scorbute.

Earth-Nuts, *Bulbo-Castanum;*
(found in divers places of *Surry,*
near *Kingston,* and other parts)
the Rind par'd off, are eaten
crude by Rustics, with a little

Pepper;

Pepper ; but are beſt boil'd like other Roots , or in Pottage rather, and are ſweet and nouriſhing.

24. Elder, *Sambucus* ; The Flowers infus'd in *Vinegar*, grateful both to the Stomach and Taſte ; attenuate thick and viſcid Humours ; and tho' the Leaves are ſomewhat rank of Smell, and ſo not commendable in *Sallet* ; they are otherwiſe (as indeed is the intire Shrub) of the moſt ſovereign Vertue ; and the ſpring Buds and tender Leaves, excellently wholſome in Pottage at that Seaſon of the Year. See *Flowers*.

25. Endive, *Endivium, Intubum Sativum* ; the largeſt, whiteſt, and tendereſt Leaves beſt boil'd, and leſs crude. It is naturally Cold , profitable for hot Stomachs ; *Incisive* and opening

ing Obstructions of the Liver :
The curled is more delicate, being eaten alone, or in Composition, with the usual *Intinctus :*
It is also excellent being boil'd ;
the middle part of the Blanch'd-
Stalk separated, eats firm, and
the ampler Leaves by many
perferr'd before *Lettuce.* See
Succory.

Eschalot. See *Onions.*

26. Fennel, *Fœniculum :* The
sweetest of *Bolognia :* Aromatick,
hot, and dry ; expels Wind,
sharpens the Sight, and recreates
the Brain ; especially the tender
Umbella and Seed-Pods. The
Stalks are to be peel'd when
young, and then dress'd like *Sellery.* The tender Tufts and
Leaves emerging, being minc'd,
are eaten alone with *Vinegar,* or
Oyl, and *Pepper,* and to correct
the colder Materials, enter properly

perly into Compofition. The *Italians* eat the blanch'd Stalk (which they call *Cartucci*) all Winter long. There is a very fmall *Green-Worm*, which fometimes lodges in the Stemm of this Plant, which is to be taken out, as the *Red* one in that of *Sellery.*

27. Flowers, *Flores* ; chiefly of the *Aromatick Efculents* and Plants are preferrable, as generally endow'd with the Vertues of their *Simples*, in a more intenfe degree ; and may therefore be eaten alone in their proper *Vehicles*, or Compofition with other *Salleting*, fprinkl'd among them ; But give a more palatable Relifh, being Infus'd in *Vinegar* ; Efpecially thofe of the *Clove-Gillyflower*, *Elder*, *Orange*, *Cowflip*, *Rofemary*, *Arch-Angel*, *Saye*, *Nafturtium Indicum*, &c. Some of them are Pickl'd, and divers

divers of them make alfo very pleafant and wholfome *Theas*, as do likewife the Wild *Time*, *Bug-lofs*, *Mint*, &c.

28. Garlick, *Allium* ; dry towards Excefs ; and tho' both by *Spaniards* and *Italians*, and the more Southern People, familiarly eaten, with almoft every thing, and efteem'd of fuch fingular Vertue to help Concoction, and thought a Charm againft all Infection and Poyfon (by which it has obtain'd the Name of the *Country man's Theriacle*) we yet think it more proper for our Northern Ruftics, efpecially living in *Uliginous* and moift places, or fuch as ufe the *Sea :* Whilft we abfolutely forbid it entrance into our *Salleting*, by reafon of its intolerable Ranknefs, and which made it fo detefted of old ; that the eating of it was (as we read) part of the Punifhment for fuch as had committed
mitted

mitted the horrid'st Crimes. To be sure, 'tis not for Ladies Palats, nor those who court them, farther than to permit a light touch on the Dish, with a *Clove* thereof, much better supply'd by the gentler *Roccombo.*

Note, That in *Spain* they sometimes eat it boil'd, which taming its fierceness, turns it into Nourishment, or rather *Medicine.*

Ginny-Pepper, *Capsicum.* See *Pepper.*

29. Goats-beard, *Trago-pogon :* The *Root* is excellent even in *Sallet,* and very Nutritive, exceeding profitable for the Breast, and may be stew'd and dress'd as *Scorzonera.*

30. Hops, *Lupulus :* Hot and moist, rather *Medicinal,* than fit for *Sallet* ; the *Buds* and young *Tendrels* excepted, which may be eaten

eaten raw ; but more conveni-
ently being boil'd, and cold like
Asparagus : They are *Diuretic* ;
depurate the Blood, and open Ob-
ſtructions.

31. Hyſſop, *Hyſſopus* ; *Thymus
Capitatus Creticus* ; *Majoran, Ma-
ry-gold,* &c. as all hot, ſpicy
Aromatics, (commonly growing
in *Kitchin-Gardens*) are of Faculty to Comfort , and ſtreng-
then ; prevalent againſt Melancholy and Phlegm : Plants, like
theſe, going under the Names of
Pot-Herbs, are much more proper for *Broths* and *Decoctions,*
than the tender *Sallet :* Yet the
Tops and *Flowers* reduc'd to Powder, are by ſome reſerv'd for
Strewings, upon the colder Ingredients ; communicating no
ungrateful Fragrancy.

32. Jack-by-the-Hedge, *Allia-
ria,* or *Sauce-alone* ; has many
Me-

Medicinal Properties, and is eaten as other *Sallets*, especially by Country People, growing wild under their Banks and Hedges.

33. Leeks, and *Cibbols*, *Porrum*; hot, and of Vertue Prolifick; since *Latona*, the Mother of *Apollo* long'd after them: The *Welch*, who eat them much, are observ'd to be very fruitful: They are also friendly to the Lungs and Stomach, being sod in Milk; a few therefore of the slender and green Summities, a little shred, do not amiss in Composition. See *Onion*.

34. Lettuce, *Lactuca:* Tho' by *Metaphor* call'd * *Mortuorum Cibi*, (to say nothing of † *Adonis*

---

* Eubulus.

† In *Lactuca* occultatum à Venere Adonin cecinit *Callimachus*, quod Allegoricè interpretatus *Athenæus* illuc referendum putat, quod in Venerem hebetiores fiant *Lactucis* vescentes assiduè.

and

and his sad *Mistriss*) by reason
of its *Soporiferous* quality, ever
was, and still continues the principal Foundation of the universal *Tribe* of *Sallets* ; which is to
Cool and Refresh, besides its o-
ther Properties : And therefore
in such high esteem with the
Ancients ; that divers of the *Va-
lerian* Family, dignify'd and eno-
bled their Name with that of
Lactucinii.

It is indeed of Nature more
cold and moist than any of the
rest ; yet less astringent, and so
harmless that it may safely be
eaten raw in Fevers ; for it allays
Heat, bridles Choler, extinguishes
Thirst, excites Appetite, kindly
Nourishes, and above all repres-
ses Vapours, conciliates Sleep,
mitigates Pain ; besides the effect it has upon the Morals, *Temperance* and *Chastity. Galen* (whose
beloved *Sallet* it was) from its
pinguid, subdulcid and agreeable
Na-

Nature, says it breeds the most laudable Blood. No marvel then that they were by the Ancients called *Sana,* by way of eminency, and so highly valu'd by the great * *Augustus,* that attributing his Recovery of a dangerous Sickness to them, 'tis reported, he erected a *Statue,* and built an *Altar* to this noble Plant. And that the most abstemious and excellent Emperor † *Tacitus* (spending almost nothing at his frugal Table in other Dainties) was yet so great a Friend to *Lettuce,* that he was us'd to say of his Prodigality, *Somnum se mercari illa sumptus effusione.* How it was celebrated by *Galen* we have heard; how he us'd it he tells himself; namely, beginning with

---

* Apud Sueton.
† Vopiscus Tacit. *For the rest both of the Kinds and Vertues of* Lettuce, *See* Plin. H. Nat. l. xix. c. 8. *and* xx, c. 7. Fernel. *&c.*

Lettuce

Lettuce in his younger Days, and concluding with it when he grew old, and that to his great advantage. In a word, we meet with nothing among all our crude Materials and *Sallet* store, so proper to mingle with any of the rest, nor so wholsome to be eaten alone, or in Composition, moderately, and with the usual *Ox olæum* of *Vinegar*, *Pepper*, and *Oyl*, &c. which last does not so perfectly agree with the *Alphange*, to which the Juice of *Orange*, or *Limon* and *Sugar* is more desirable : *Aristoxenus* is reported to have irrigated his *Lettuce*-Beds with an *Oinomelite*, or mixture of *Wine* and *Honey* : And certainly 'tis not for nothing that our Garden-Lovers, and *Brothers of the Sallet*, have been so exceedingly Industrious to cultivate this Noble Plant, and multiply its *Species* ; for to name a few in present use : We have the *Al-*

D   *phange*

phange of *Montpelier*, crisp and delicate ; the *Arabic* ; *Amber-velleres* ; *Belgrade, Cabbage, Ca-puchin, Cross-Lettuce, Curl'd* ; the *Genoa* (lasting all the Winter) the *Imperial, Lambs*, or *Agnine*, and *Lobbs* or *Lop-Lettuces.* The *French Minion* a dwarf kind : The *Oak-Leaf, Passion, Roman, Shell*, and *Silesian*, hard and crimp (esteemed of the best and rarest) with divers more : And here let it be noted, that besides three or four sorts of this Plant, and some few of the rest, there was within our remembrance, rarely any other *Salleting* serv'd up to the best Tables ; with unblanch'd *Endive, Succory, Purselan*, (and indeed little other variety) *Sugar* and *Vinegar* being the constant *Vehicles* (without *Oyl*) but now *Sugar* is almost wholly banish'd from all, except the more effe-minate Palates, as too much pal-ling, and taking from the grate-ful

ful *Acid* now in ufe, tho' other-
wife not totally to be reproved:
Lettuce boil'd and *Condited* is
fometimes fpoken of.

35. Limon, *Limonia, citrea ma-
la*; exceedingly refrefhing, *Cordial*, &c. The Pulp being blended with the Juice, fecluding the
over-fweet or bitter. See *O-
range*.

36. Mallow, *Malva*; the
curl'd, emollient, and friendly
to the *Ventricle*, and fo rather
Medicinal; yet may the Tops,
well boil'd, be admitted, and the
reft (tho' out of ufe at pre-
fent) was taken by the Poets
for all *Sallets* in general. *Pythagoras* held *Malvæ folium Sanctif-
fimum*; and we find *Epimenides*
in * *Plato* at his *Mallows* and
Afphodel; and indeed it was of

---

* De Legib.

old

old the first Dish at Table : The
Romans had it also *in deliciis,*
¶ *Malvæ salubres corpori,* approved by * *Galen* and † *Dioscorides* ; namely the *Garden-
Mallow,* by others the *Wild* ;
but I think both proper rather
for the *Pot,* than *Sallet.* *Nonius*
supposes the tall *Rosea, Arbore-
scent Holi-hocks* that bears the
broad Flower, for the best, and
very ‖ *Laxative* ; but by reason
of their clamminess and *Lentor,*
banished from our *Sallet,* tho'
by some commended and eaten

¶ *Hor.* Epod. 11.
* De Simp. Medic. *L.* vii.
† *Lib.* ii. *cap.* 3.
‖ Exoneraturas Ventrem mihi Villica Malvas
  Attulit, & varias, quas habet hortus. Opes.
             Mart. Lib. x.

    And our sweet Poet :
—————Nulla est humanior herba,
Nulla magis suavi commoditate bona est,
Omnia tam placidè regerat, blandéque relaxat,
Emollítque vias, nec sinit esse rudes.
            Cowl. *Plan. L.* 4.

               with

with *Oyl* and *Vinegar*, and some
with *Butter*.

Mercury, *Bonus Henricus*,
English Mercury, or *Lapathum
Unctuosum.* See *Blitum.*

37. Melon, *Melo* ; to have
been reckon'd rather among
Fruits ; and tho' an usual Ingredient in our *Sallet* ; yet for its
transcendent delicacy and flavor,
cooling and exhilarating Nature
(if sweet, dry, weighty, and
well-fed) not only superior to
all the *Gourd*-kind, but Paragon
with the noblest Productions of
the Garden. *Jos. Scaliger* and
Casaubon, think our *Melon* unknown to the Ancients, (which
others contradict) as yet under
the name of *Cucumers* : But he
who reads how artificially they
were Cultivated, rais'd under
Glasses, and expos'd to the hot
Sun, (for *Tiberius*) cannot well

D 3   doubt

doubt of their being the same
with ours.

There is also a *Winter-Melon*,
large and with black Seeds, exceedingly Cooling, brought us
from abroad, and the hotter
Climates, where they drink *Water* after eating *Melons*; but in
the colder (after all dispute)
Wine is judg'd the better : That
it has indeed by some been accus'd as apt to corrupt in the Stomach (as do all things else eaten
in excess) is not deny'd : But a
perfect good *Melon* is certainly as
harmless a Fruit as any whatsoever ; and may safely be mingl'd
with *Sallet*, in Pulp or Slices, or
more properly eaten by it self,
with a little *Salt* and *Pepper* ; for
a *Melon* which requires *Sugar* to
commend it, wants of Perfection.
Note, That this Fruit was very
rarely cultivated in *England*, so
as to bring it to Maturity, till
Sir *Geo. Gardner* came out of
Spain

Spain. I my self remembring, when an ordinary *Melon* would have been sold for five or six Shillings. The small unripe Fruit, when the others are past, may be Pickl'd with *Mango*, and are very delicate.

38. Mint, *Mentha*; the *Angustifolia Spicata*, Spear-Mint; dry and warm, very fragrant, a little press'd, is friendly to the weak Stomach, and powerful against all *Nervous* Crudities: The gentler Tops of the *Orange-Mint*, enter well into our Composition, or are grateful alone (as are also the other sorts) with the Juice of *Orange*, and a little *Sugar*.

39. Mushroms, *Fungi*; By the * Orator call'd *Terræ*, by *Porphyry Deorum filii*, without Seed (as

* Cic. *ad* Attic.

produc'd by the Midwifry of
Autumnal Thunder-Storms, por-
tending the Mifchief they caufe)
by the *French*, *Champignons*,
with all the Species of the
Boletus, &c. for being, as fome
hold, neither *Root*, *Herb*, *Flower*,
nor *Fruit*, nor to be eaten crude;
fhould be therefore banifh'd en-
try into our *Sallet*, were I to
order the Compofition; however fo highly contended for by
many, as the very principal and
top of all the reft; whilft I think
them tolerable only (at leaft in
this *Climate*) if being frefh and
skilfully chofen, they are accommodated with the niceft Care and
Circumfpection; generally reported to have fomething malignant and noxious in them:
Nor without caufe; from the
many fad Examples, frequent
Mifchiefs, and funeft Accidents
they have produc'd, not only to
particular Perfons, but whole
Fa-

Families : Exalted indeed they were to the second Course of the *Cæsarian Tables*, with the noble Title Βρῶμα Θεῶν, a Dainty fit for the *Gods* alone ; to whom they sent the Emperor *Claudius*, as they have many since, to the other World. But he that reads how *Seneca* ∴ deplores his lost Friend, that brave Commander *Annæus Serenus*, and several other gallant Persons with him, who all of them perish'd at the same Repast ; would be apt to ask with the † *Naturalist* (speaking of this suspicious Dainty) *Quæ voluptas tanta ancipitis cibi?* and who indeed would hazard it ? So true is that of the Poet ; He that eats *Mushroms*, many times *Nil amplius edit*, eats no more perhaps

---

* Sueton. *in Claudi.*
∴ Sen. Ep. lxiii.
† Plin. N. H. *l.* xxi . c. 2 ;.

all

all his Life after. What other deterring *Epithets* are given for our Caution, Βάρη πνιγόεντα μυκήτων, *heavy* and *choaking*. (*Athenæus* reporting of the Poet *Euripides*'s, finding a Woman and her three Children strangl'd by eating of them) one would think sufficient warning.

Among these comes in the *Fungus Reticularis*, to be found about *London*, as at *Fulham* and other places; whilst at no small charge we send for them into *France*; as we also do for *Trufles*, *Peg-nuts*, and other subterraneous *Tubera*, which in *Italy* they fry in Oyl, and eat with *Pepper:* They are commonly discovered by a *Nasute Swine* purposely brought up; being of a Chesnut Colour, and heady Smell, and not seldom found in *England*, particularly in a Park of my Lord *Cotton*'s, at *Rushton* or *Rusbery* in *Northampton*-shire, and doubtless

in

in other † places too were they
fought after. How thefe rank
and provocative Excrefcences are
to be ‖treated (of themfelves in-
fipid enough, and only famous
for their kindly taking any Pickle
or *Conditure*) that they may do
the lefs Mifchief, we might here
fet down. But fince there be fo
many ways of Dreffing them,
that I can incourage none to ufe
them, for Reafons given (befides
that they do not at all concern
our fafer and innocent *Sallet* Furniture) I forbear it; and referr
thofe who long after this beloved
Ragout, and other *Voluptuaria
Venena* (as *Seneca* calls them) to
what our Learned Dr. *Lyfter** fays
of the many Venomous *Infects*
harbouring and corrupting in a

‖ Apitius, *lib.* vii. *cap.* 13.
† Tranfact. Philof. *Num.* 202.
* Philof. Tranfact. *Num.* 89. *Journey to*
Paris.

new

new found-out Species of *Mushroms* had lately *in deliciis.* Those,
in the mean time, which are e-
steemed best, and less pernicious,
(of which see the *Appendix*)
are such as rise in rich, airy, and
dry † Pasture-Grounds; growing
on the Staff or *Pedicule* of about
an Inch thick and high; moderately Swelling (*Target*-like)
round and firm, being under-
neath of a pale saffronish hue,
curiously radiated in parallel
Lines and Edges, which becoming either Yellow, Orange, or
Black, are to be rejected: But
besides what the Harvest-Months
produce, they are likewise rais'd
* Artificially; as at *Naples* in
their Wine-Cellars, upon an heap
of rank Earth, heaped upon a

---

† Pratensibus optima fungis Natura est:
aliis male creditur, *Hor. Sat. l.* 7. *Sat.* 4.
  * Bacon *Nat. Hist.* 12. Cent. vii. 547, 548,
&c.

cer-

certain supposed *Stone*, but in truth, (as the curious and noble * *Peiresky* tells us, he found to be) nothing but an heap of old *Fungus*'s, reduc'd and compacted to a stony hardness, upon which they lay Earth, and sprinkle it with warm Water, in which *Mushroms* have been steeped. And in *France*, by making an hot Bed of *Asses*-Dung, and when the heat is in Temper, watering it (as above) well impregnated with the Parings and Offals of refuse *Fungus*'s; and such a Bed will last two or three Years, and sometimes our common *Melon*-Beds afford them, besides other Experiments.

40. Mustard, *Sinapi*; exceeding hot and *mordicant*, not only

---

* Gassend. *Vita Peirs.* l. iv. Raderus *Mart.* l. Epig. xlvi. In ponticum, *says, within four Days.*

in the Seed but Leaf alſo; eſpecially in *Seedling* young Plants,
like thoſe of *Radiſhes* (newly
peeping out of the Bed) is
of incomparable effect to quicken
and revive the Spirits; ſtreng-
thening the Memory, expelling
heavineſs, preventing the Verti-
ginous Palſie, and is a laudable
Cephalick. Beſides it is an ap-
prov'd *Antiſcorbutick;* aids Concoction, cuts and diſſipates Phleg-
matick Humours. In ſhort, 'tis
the moſt noble *Embamma,* and
ſo neceſſary an Ingredient to all
cold and raw *Salleting,* that it is
very rarely, if at all, to be left
out. In *Italy* in making
Muſtard, they mingle *Limon* and
*Orange-*Peel, with the Seeds. How
the beſt is made, ſee hereafter.

Naſturtium Indicum. See *Creſſes.*

41. Nettles, *Urtica;* Hot, dry,
Diuretic, Solvent; purifies the
Blood:

Blood: The Buds, and very tender *Cimæ*, a little bruised, are by some eaten raw, by others boil'd, especially in *Spring-Pottage*, with other Herbs.

42. Onion, *Cepa*, *Porrum*; the best are such as are brought us out of *Spain*, whence they of St. *Omers* had them, and some that have weigh'd eight Pounds. Choose therefore the large, round, white, and thin Skin'd. Being eaten crude and alone with *Oyl*, *Vinegar*, and *Pepper*, we own them in *Sallet*, not so hot as *Garlick*, nor at all so rank: Boil'd, they give a kindly relish; raise Appetite, corroborate the Stomach, cut Phlegm, and profit the *Asthmatical* : But eaten in excess, are said to offend the Head and Eyes, unless *Edulcorated* with a gentle maceration. In the mean time, as to their being noxious to the Sight, is imputable only

to

to the Vapour rifing from the raw Onion, when peeled, which fome commend for its purging and quickning that Senfe. How they are us'd in Pottage, boil'd in Milk, ftew'd, *&c.* concerns the Kitchin. In our cold *Sallet* we fupply them with the *Porrum Sectile,* Tops of *Leeks,* and *Efchalots (Afcalonia)* of guft more exalted, yet not to the degree of *Garlick.* Or (by what of later ufe is much preferr'd) with a *Clove* or two of *Raccombo,* of a yet milder and delicate nature, which by rubbing the Difh only, imparts its Vertue agreeably e-nough. In *Italy* they frequently make a *Sallet* of *Scalions, Cives,* and *Chibbols* only feafon'd with *Oyl* and *Pepper;* and an honeft laborious Country-man, with good *Bread, Salt,* and a little *Parfley,* will make a contented Meal with a roafted *Onion.* How this noble *Bulb* was deified in
* *Egypt*

* *Egypt* we are told, and that whilst they were building the *Pyramids*, there was spent in this Root † *Ninety Tun* of *Gold* among the Workmen. So lushious and tempting it seems they were, that as whole Nations have subsisted on them alone; so the *Israelites* were ready to return to *Slavery* and *Brick-making* for the love of them. Indeed *Hecamedes* we find presents them to *Patroclus*, in *Homer*, as a *Regalo*; But certainly we are either mistaken in the *Species* (which some will have to be *Melons*) or use *Poetick* Licence, when we so highly magnify them.

43. Orach, *Atriplex* : Is cooling, allays the *Pituit* Humor : Being set over the Fire, neither

---

* O Sanctas gentes, quibus hæc nascuntur in Numina. —— *Juv. Sat.* 15.   (hortis
† Herodotus.

this, nor *Lettuce*, needs any other Water than their own moisture to boil them in, without Expression: The tender Leaves are mingl'd with other cold *Salleting*; but 'tis better in Pottage. See *Blitum*.

44. Orange, *Arantiæ* (*Malum aureum*) moderately dry, cooling, and incisive; sharpens Appetite, exceedingly refreshes and resits Putrefaction: We speak of the *Sub acid*; the sweet and bitter *Orange* being of no use in our *Sallet*. The *Limon* is somewhat more acute, cooling and extinguishing Thirst; of all the Ὀξύβαφα the best *succedaneum* to *Vinegar*. The very Spoils and Rinds of *Orange* and *Limon* being shred and sprinkl'd among the other Herbs, correct the Acrimony. But they are the tender *Seedlings* from the *Hot-Bed*, which impart an *Aromatic* exceed-

ceedingly grateful to the Stomach. *Vide* Limon.

45. Parſnep, *Paſtinaca*, Carrot;
firſt boil'd, being cold, is of it
ſelf a Winter-*Sallet*, eaten with
Oyl, *Vinegar*, &c. and having
ſomething of Spicy, is by ſome,
thought more nouriſhing than
the *Turnep*.

46. Peaſe, *Piſum*; the *Pod* of
the *Sugar-Peaſe*, when firſt beginning to appear, with the
Husk and *Tendrels*, affording a
pretty *Acid*, enter into the Compoſition, as do thoſe of *Hops* and
the *Vine*.

47. Peper, *Piper*; hot and
dry in a high degree; of ap-
prov'd Vertue againſt all flatulency proceeding from cold and
phlegmatic Conſtitutions, and
generally all Crudities whatſoe-
ver; and therefore for being of
E 2   uni-

universal use to correct and temper the cooler Herbs, and such as abound in moisture; It is a never to be omitted Ingredient of our *Sallets*; provided it be not too minutely beaten (as oft we find it) to an almost impalpable Dust, which is very pernicious, and frequently adheres and sticks in the folds of the Stomach, where, instead of promoting Concoction, it often causes a *Cardialgium*, and fires the Blood: It should therefore be grosly contus'd only.

Indian Capsicum, superlatively hot and burning, is yet by the *Africans* eaten with *Salt* and *Vinegar* by it self, as an usual Condiment; but wou'd be of dangerous consequence with us; being so much more of an acrimonious and terribly biting quality, Which by Art and Mixture is notwithstanding render'd not only safe, but very agreeable in our *Sallet*.　　　　Take

Take the *Pods*, and dry them well in a Pan; and when they are become sufficiently hard, cut them into small pieces, and stamp 'em in a Mortar to dust: To each Ounce of which add a Pound of *Wheat-flour*, fermented with a little *Levain :* Kneed and make them into Cakes or Loaves cut long-wise, in shape of *Naples-Biscuit.* These Re-bake a second time, till they are Stone-hard : Pound them again as before, and serce it through a fine Sieve, for a very proper Seasoning, instead of vulgar *Peper.* The Mordicancy thus allay'd, be sure to make the Mortar very clean, after having beaten *Indian Capsicum,* before you stamp any thing in it else. The green Husks, or first peeping Buds of the *Walnut-*Tree, dry'd to Powder, serve for *Peper* in some places, and so do *Myrtle berries.*

E 3 48. Persley,

48. Persley, *Petroselinum*, or *Apium hortense*; being hot and dry, opens Obstructions, is very *Diuretic*, yet nourishing, *edulcorated* in shifted warm Water (the Roots especially) but of less Vertue than *Alexanders*; nor so convenient in our crude *Sallet*, as when decocted on a Medicinal Account. Some few tops of the tender Leaves may yet be admitted; tho' it was of old, we read, never brought to the Table at all, as sacred to *Oblivium* and the *Defunct*. In the mean time, there being nothing more proper for Stuffing, (*Farces*) and other *Sauces*, we consign it to the *Olitories*. Note, that *Persley* is not so hurtful to the Eyes as is reported. See *Sellery*.

49. Pimpernel, *Pimpinella*; eaten by the *French* and *Italians*, is our common *Burnet*; of so chear-

chearing and exhilarating a quality, and so generally commended,
as (giving it admittance into all
Sallets) 'tis pass'd into a Proverb :

*L' Insalata non è buon, ne bella,
Ove non è la Pimpinella.*

But a fresh sprig in *Wine*, recom-
mends it to us as its most genuine
Element.

50. Purslain, *Portulaca*; especially the *Golden* whilst tender,
next the Seed-leaves, with the
young Stalks, being eminently
moist and cooling, quickens Appetite, asswages Thirst, and is
very profitable for hot and *Bilious* Tempers, as well as *Sanguine*,
and generally entertain'd in all
our *Sallets*, mingled with the
hotter Herbs : 'Tis likewise familiarly eaten alone with *Oyl* and

E 4   *Vine-*

Vinegar ; but with moderation, as having been sometimes found to corrupt in the Stomach, which being *Pickl'd* 'tis not so apt to do. Some eat it cold, after it has been boil'd, which Dr. *Muffet* would have in *Wine*, for Nourishment.

The Shrub *Halimus*, is a sort of *Sea-Purslain* : The newly peeping Leaves (tho' rarely us'd) afford a no unpleasant *Acidulæ*, even during Winter, if it prove not too severe.

Purslain is accus'd for being hurtful to the *Teeth*, if too much eaten.

51. Radish, *Raphanus.* Albeit rather Medicinal, than so commendably accompanying our *Sallets* (wherein they often slice the larger Roots) are much inferior to the young Seedling Leaves and Roots ; rai-

raifed on the * Monthly *Hot-Bed*, almoft the whole Year round, affording a very grateful mordacity, and fufficiently attempers the cooler Ingredients: The bigger Roots (fo much defir'd) fhould be fuch as being tranfparent, eat fhort and quick, without ftringinefs, and not too biting. Thefe are eaten alone with *Salt* only, as carrying their *Peper* in them; and were indeed by *Diofcorides* and *Pliny* celebrated above all Roots whatfoever; infomuch as in the *Delphic* Temple, there was *Raphanus ex auro dicatus*, a Radifh of folid Gold; and 'tis faid of *Mofchius*, that he wrote a whole Volume in their praife. Notwithftanding all which, I am fure, the great † *Hippocrates* utterly condemns them, as *Vitiofæ*, *innatan-*

---

* ὥρα τὸ ῥᾳδίας φαίνεσθαι, quia tertio à fatu die appareat.

† De diæta *lib*. ii. *cap*. 25.

tes ac ægre concoctiles. And the *Naturalist* calls it *Cibus Illiberalis*, fitter for *Rustics* than *Gentlemens* Tables. And indeed (besides that they decay the Teeth) experience tells us, that as the Prince of *Physicians* writes, It is hard of Digestion, *Inimicous* to the Stomach, causing nauseous Eructations, and sometimes Vomiting, tho' otherwise *Diuretic*, and thought to repel the Vapours of *Wine*, when the *Wits* were at their genial *Club.* *Dioscorides* and † *Galen* differ about their Eating; One prescribes it before Meals, the latter for after. Some macerate the young Roots in warm Milk, to render them more *Nourishing.*

There is a *Raphanus rusticanus,* the *Spanish* black *Horse-Radish,* of a hotter quality, and not so

---

† De Aliment. Facult. *lib.* ii.

friendly

friendly to the Head; but a notable *Antiscorbutic*, which may be eaten all the Winter, and on that account an excellent Ingredient in the Composition of *Mustard*; as are also the thin Shavings, mingled with our cold Herbs. And now before I have done with this Root, for an excellent and universal *Condiment*. Take *Horse-Radish*, whilst newly drawn out of the Earth, otherwise laid to steep in Water a competent time; then *grate* it on a *Grater* which has no bottom, that so it may pass thro', like a Mucilage, into a Dish of Earthen Ware: This temper'd with *Vinegar*, in which a little *Sugar* has been dissolv'd, you have a *Sauce* supplying *Mustard* to the *Sallet*, and serving likewise for any Dish besides.

52. *Ram-*

52. Rampion, *Rapunculus*, or the *Esculent Campanula:* The tender Roots eaten in the Spring, like those of *Radishes*, but much more Nourishing.

53. Rocket, *Eruca Spanish*; hot and dry, to be qualified with *Lettuce*, *Purcelain*, and the rest, &c. See *Tarragon*.

Roccombo. See *Onions*.

54. Rosemary, *Rosmarinus*; Soverainly *Cephalic*, and for the *Memory*, *Sight*, and *Nerves*, incomparable: And tho' not us'd in the Leaf with our *Sallet* furniture, yet the *Flowers*, a little bitter, are always welcome in *Vinegar*; but above all, a fresh Sprig or two in a Glass of *Wine*. See *Flowers*.

55. Sage,

55. Sage, *Salvia*; hot and dry. The tops of the *Red*, well pick'd and wash'd (being often defil'd with Venomous Slime, and almost imperceptible *Insects*) with the *Flowers*, retain all the noble Properties of the other hot Plants; more especially for the *Head*, *Memory*, *Eyes*, and all *Paralytical* Affections. In short, 'tis a Plant endu'd with so many and wonderful Properties, as that the assiduous use of it is said to render Men *Immortal:* We cannot therefore but allow the tender *Summities* of the young Leaves; but principally the *Flowers* in our cold *Sallet*; yet so as not to domineer.

Salsifax, *Scorzonera*. See *Vipergrass*.

56. Sampier, *Crithmum:* That growing on the Sea-Cliffs (as

about

about *Dover*, &c.) not only *Pickl'd*, but crude and cold, when young and tender (and such as we may Cultivate, and have in our *Kitchin-Gardens*, almost the Year round) is in my Opinion, for its *Aromatic*, and other excellent Vertues and Effects against the *Spleen*, Cleansing the Passages, sharpning Appetite, *&c.* so far preferrable to most of our hotter Herbs, and *Sallet*-Ingredients, that I have long wonder'd, it has not been long since propagated in the *Potagene*, as it is in *France* ; from whence I have often receiv'd the Seeds, which have prosper'd better, and more kindly with me, than what comes from our own Coasts : It does not indeed *Pickle* so well, as being of a more tender Stalk and Leaf : But in all other respects for composing *Sallets*, it has nothing like it.

57. Sca-

57. Scalions, *Afcalonia, Cepæ*; The *French* call them *Appetites*, which it notably quickens and ftirs up: Corrects Crudities, and promotes Concoction. The *Italians* fteep them in Water, mince, and eat them cold with *Oyl, Vinegar, Salt*, &c.

58. Scurvy-grafs, *Cochlearia*, of the Garden, but efpecially that of the Sea, is fharp, biting, and hot; of Nature like *Nafturtium*, prevalent in the *Scorbute*. A few of the tender Leaves may be admitted in our Compofition. See *Nafturtium Indicum*.

59. Sellery, *Apium Italicum*, (and of the *Petrofeline* Family) was formerly a ftranger with us (nor very long fince in *Italy*) is an hot and more generous fort of *Macedonian Perfley*, or *Smallage*. The tender Leaves of the *Blancht*

Stalk

Stalk do well in our *Sallet*, as likewise the slices of the whiten'd Stems, which being crimp and short, first peel'd and slit long wise, are eaten with *Oyl*, *Vinegar*, *Salt*, and *Peper* ; and for its high and grateful Taste, is ever plac'd in the middle of the *Grand Sallet*, at our Great Mens Tables, and *Prætors* Feasts, as the Grace of the whole Board. *Caution* is to be given of a small red *Worm*, often lurking in these Stalks, as does the green in *Fennil*.

Shallots.   See *Onion.*

60. Skirrets, *Sifarum* ; hot and moist, corroborating, and good for the Stomach, exceedingly nourishing, wholsome and delicate ; of all the *Root-kind*, not subject to be Windy, and so valued by the Emperor *Tiberius*, that he accepted them for Tribute.

This

This excellent Root is seldom eaten raw; but being boil'd, stew'd, roasted under the Embers, bak'd in Pies, whole, sliced, or in pulp, is very acceptable to all Palates. 'Tis reported they were heretofore something bitter; See what Culture and Education effects!

61. Sorrel, *Acetosa*: of which there are divers kinds. The *French Acetocella*, with the round Leaf, growing plentifully in the *North* of *England*; *Roman Oxalis*; the broad *German*, &c. but the best is of *Green-Land*: by nature Cold, Abstersive, Acid, sharpning Appetite, asswages Heat, cools the Liver, strengthens the Heart; is an *Antiscorbutic*, resisting Putrefaction, and imparting so grateful a quickness to the rest, as supplies the want of *Orange*, *Limon*, and other *Omphacia*, and therefore never

to

to be excluded. Vide *Wood-Sorrel.*

62. Sow-thistle, *Sonchus*; of the *Intybus*-kind. *Galen* was us'd to eat it as *Lettuce*; exceedingly welcome to the late *Morocco* Ambassador and his Retinue.

63. Sparagus, *Asparagus* (*ab Asperitate*) temperately hot, and moist; *Cordial, Diuretic,* easie of Digestion, and next to *Flesh,* nothing more nourishing, as *Sim. Sethius,* an excellent Physician holds. They are sometimes, but very seldom, eaten raw with *Oyl,* and *Vinegar*; but with more delicacy (the bitterness first exhausted) being so speedily boil'd, as not to lose the *verdure* and agreeable tenderness; which is done by letting the Water boil, before you put them in. I do not esteem the *Dutch* great and
larger

larger fort (efpecially rais'd by
the ranknefs of the Beds) fo
fweet and agreeable, as thofe of
a moderate fize.

64. Spinach, *Spinachia*: of old
not us'd in *Sallets*, and the oft-
ner kept out the better ; I fpeak
of the *crude* : But being boil'd
to a *Pult*, and without other
Water than its own moifture, is
a moft excellent Condiment with
Butter, *Vinegar*, or *Limon*, for
almoft all forts of boil'd Flefh,
and may accompany a Sick Man's
Diet. 'Tis *Laxative* and *Emollient*,
and therefore profitable for the
Aged, and (tho' by original a
Spaniard) may be had at almoft
any Seafon, and in all places.

Stone-Crop, *Sedum Minus*.
See *Trick-Madame*.

65. Succory, *Cichorium*, an *Intube*; erratic and wild, with a narrow dark Leaf, different from the *Sative*, tho' probably by culture only; and for being very bitter, a little *edulcorated* with *Sugar* and *Vinegar*, is by some eaten in the Summer, and more grateful to the Stomach than the Palate. See *Endive*.

66. Tanfy, *Tanacetum*; hot and cleanfing; but in regard of its domineering relifh, fparingly mixt with our cold *Sallet*, and much fitter (tho' in very fmall quantity) for the Pan, being qualified with the Juices of other fresh Herbs, *Spinach*, *Green Corn*, *Violet*, *Primrofe-Leaves*, &c. at entrance of the Spring, and then fried brownifh. is eaten hot with the Juice of *Orange* and *Sugar*, as one of the moft agreeable of all the boil'd *Herbaceous* Difhes.

67. Tar-

67. **Tarragon,** *Draco Herba,*
of *Spanish* Extraction ; hot and
spicy : The Tops and young
Shoots, like those of *Rochet,* never to be secluded our Composition, especially where there is
much *Lettuce.* 'Tis highly cordial and friendly to the Head,
Heart, Liver, correcting the weak-
ness of the Ventricle, *&c.*

68. **Thistle,** *Carduus Mariæ* ;
our Lady's milky or dappl'd
Thistle, disarm'd of its Prickles,
is worth esteem : The young
Stalk about *May,* being peel'd
and soak'd in Water, to extract
the bitterness, boil'd or raw, is a
very wholsome *Sallet,* eaten with
Oyl, Salt, and *Peper :* some eat
them sodden in proper Broath,
or bak'd in Pies, like the *Arti-*
choak ; but the tender Stalk boil'd
or fry'd, some preferr; both Nourishing and Restorative.

F 3   69. Trick-

69. Trick-Madame, *Sedum minus*, Stone-Crop; is cooling and moist, grateful to the Stomach. The *Cimata* and Tops, when young and tender, dress'd as *Purselane*, is a frequent Ingredient in our cold *Sallet*.

70. Turnep, *Rapum*; moderately hot and moist: *Napus*; the long *Navet* is certainly the most delicate of them, and best Nourishing. *Pliny* speaks of no fewer than six sorts, and of several Colours; some of which were suspected to be artificially tinged. But with us, the yellow is preferr'd; by others the red *Bohemian*. But of whatever kind, being sown upon the *Hot-bed*, and no bigger than seedling *Radish*, they do excellently in Composition; as do also the Stalks of the common *Turnep*, when first beginning to Bud.

And

And here should not be forgotten, that wholsome, as well as agreeable sort of *Bread*, we are * taught to make; and of which we have eaten at the greatest Persons Tables, hardly to be distinguish'd from the best of *Wheat*.

Let the *Turneps* first be peel'd, and boil'd in Water till soft and tender; then strongly pressing out the Juice, mix them together, and when dry (beaten or pounded very fine) with their weight of *Wheat*-Meal, season it as you do other *Bread*, and knead it up; then letting the Dough remain a little to *ferment*, fashion the Paste into Loaves, and bake it like common Bread.

Some roast *Turneps* in a Paper under the Embers, and eat them with *Sugar* and *Butter*.

---

* *Philos. Transact.* Vol. xvii. Num. 205. p. 970.

71. Vine, *Vitis*, the *Capreols*, *Tendrels*, and *Claspers* (like those of the *Hop*, &c.) whilst very young, have an agreeable *Acid*, which may be eaten alone, or with other *Sallet*.

72. Viper-grass, *Tragopogon*, *Scorzonera*, *Salsifex*, &c. tho' Medicinal, and excellent against the *Palpitation of the Heart*, *Faintings*, *Obstruction of the Bowels*, &c. are besides a very sweet and pleasant *Sallet*; being laid to soak out the bitterness, then peel'd, may be eaten raw, or *Condited*; but best of all stew'd with *Marrow*, *Spice*, *Wine*, &c. as *Artichoak*, *Skirrets*, &c. sliced or whole. They likewise may bake, fry, or boil them; a more excellent Root there is hardly growing.

73. Wood-

73. Wood-Sorrel, *Trifolium acetofum*, or *Alleluja*, of the nature of other *Sorrels*.

To all which might we add fundry more, formerly had in *deliciis*, fince grown *obfolete* or quite neglected with us : As among the nobleft *Bulbs*, that of the *Tulip* ; a Root of which has been valued not to eat, but for the *Flower* (and yet eaten by miftake) at more than an hundred Pounds. The young frefh *Bulbs* are fweet and high of tafte.

The *Afphodil* or *Daffodil*; a *Sallet* fo rare in *Hefiod*'s Days, that *Lobel* thinks it the *Parfnep*, tho' not at all like it ; however it was (with the *Mallow*) taken anciently for any *Edule*-Root.

The *Ornithogalons* roafted, as they do *Cheftnuts*, are eaten by the *Italians*, the wild yellow efpe-

especially, with *Oyl*, *Vinegar*, and
Peper. And so the small *tuberous*
Roots of *Gramen Amygdalosum*,
which they also roast, and make
an *Emulsion* of, to use in Broaths
as a great Restorative. The *Oxy-*
lapathum, not us'd of old; in the
time of *Galen* was eaten frequently. As also *Dracontium*, with
the Mordicant *Arum Theophrasti*,
which *Dodonæus* teaches how to
Dress. Nay, divers of the *Satyrions*,
which some condited with *Sugar*,
others boil'd in Milk for a great
Nourisher, now discarded. But
what think we of the *Cicuta*,
which there are who reckon a-
mong *Sallet* Herbs? But whatever it is in any other Country,
'tis certainly Mortiferous in ours.
To these add the *Viola Matrona-*
lis , *Radix Lunaria*, &c. nay,
the *Green Popy*, by most accounted among the deadly Poysons:
How cautious then ought our
Sallet-Gatherers to be, in reading
an-

ancient Authors; left they happen to be impos'd on, where they treat of Plants, that are familiarly eaten in other Countries, and among other Nations and People of more robuft and ftrong Conftitutions? befides the hazard of being miftaken in the Names of divers *Simples*, not as yet fully agreed upon among the Learned in *Botany*.

There are befides feveral remaining, which tho' *Abdicated* here with us, find Entertainment ftill in Foreign Countries: As the large *Heliotrope* and Sun-flower (e're it comes to expand, and fhew its golden Face) which being drefs'd as the *Artichoak*, is eaten for a dainty. This I add as a new Difcovery. I once made *Macaroons* with the ripe blanch'd Seeds, but the *Turpentine* did fo domineer over all, that it did not anfwer expectation. The *Radix Perfonata* mounting

ing with their young Heads.
Lysimachia siliquosa glabra minor,
when fresh and tender, begins
to come into the *Sallet*-Tribe.
The pale whiter *Popy,* is eaten by
the *Genouese.* By the *Spaniards,*
the tops of *Wormwood* with *Oyl*
alone, and without so much as
Bread ; profitable indeed to the
Stomach, but offensive to the
Head : As is also *Coriander* and
Rue, which *Galen* was accustom'd
to eat raw, and by it self, with
Oyl and *Salt,* as exceedingly grateful, as well as wholsome, and of
great vertue against Infection.
Pliny, I remember, reports it to
be of such effect for the Preservation of *Sight* ; that the *Painters*
of his Time, us'd to devour a
great quantity of it. And it is
still by the *Italians* frequently
mingled among their *Sallets.* The
Lapatha Personata (common *Bur-
dock*) comes now and then to
the best Tables, about *April,* and
when

when young, before the *Burrs* and *Clots* appear, being ftrip'd, and the bitterneſs ſoaked out, treated as the *Chardoon*, is eaten in *Poiverade*; Some alſo boil them. More might here be reckon'd up, but theſe may ſuffice; ſince as we find ſome are left off, and gone out, ſo others be introduc'd and come in their room, and that in much greater Plenty and Variety, than was ever known by our Anceſtors. The *Cucumber* it ſelf, now ſo univerſally eaten, being accounted little better than *Poyſon*, even within our Memory, as already noted.

To conclude, and after all that has been ſaid of Plants and *Salleting*, formerly in great eſteem, (but ſince obſolete and quite rejected); What if the exalted Juice of the ancient *Silphium* ſhould come in, and challenge the Precedency? It is a
* Plant

* Plant formerly so highly priz'd, and rare for the richness of its Taste and other Vertues; that as it was dedicated to *Apollo*, and hung up in his Temple at *Delphi*; So we read of one single Root brought to the Emperor *Nero* for an extraordinary Present; and the Drug so esteem'd, that the *Romans* had long before amass'd a quantity of it, and kept it in the Treasury, till *Julius Cæsar* rob'd it, and took this away, as a thing of mighty value: In a word, it was of that Account; that as a sacred Plant, those of the *Cyrenaic Africa*, honour'd the very Figure of it, by stamping it on the Reverse of their † Coin; and when they would commend a

---

* *Plin.* H. Nat. Lib. xix. cap. 3. & xx. c. 22. Seo Jo. Tzetzes Chil. vi. 48. & xvii. 119.

† Spanheim, De usu & Præst. Numis. Differt. 4to. *It was sometimes also the Reverse of* Jupiter Hammon.

thing

thing for its worth to the Skies, Βάτℓυ σίλφιον, grew into a Proverb : *Battus* having been the Founder of the City *Cyrene*, near which it only grew. 'Tis indeed contested among the Learned *Botanosophists*, whether this Plant was not the same with *Laserpitium*, and the *Laser* it yields, the odoriferous † *Benzoin* ? But doubtless had we the true and genuine *Silphium* (for it appears to have been often sophisticated, and a spurious sort brought into *Italy*) it would soon recover its pristine Reputation, and that it was not celebrated so for nothing extraordinary ; since besides its Medicinal Vertue ; it was a wonderful Corroborater of the Stomach, a Restorer of lost Appetite, and Masculine Vigour, &c.

---

† —— ȣδ ἰὰν εἰδοίης γέ μοι
Τὸν πλȣτον ἀυτὸν κỳ τὸ Βάτℓυ σίλφιον. *Aristoph.* in Pluto. Act. iv. Sc. 3.

and

and that they made use of it almost in every thing they eat.

But should we now really tell
the World, that this precious
Juice is, by many, thought to be
no other than the † *Fœtid Aſſa*;
our nicer *Sallet-Eaters* (who yet
bestow as odious an Epithet on
the vulgar *Garlick*) would cry
out upon it as intolerable, and
perhaps hardly believe it : But as
Ariſtophanes has brought it in,
and sufficiently deſcrib'd it; so
the *Scholiaſt* upon the place, puts
it out of Controverſy : And
that they made uſe both of the
Leaves, Stalk, (and *Extract* eſpecially) as we now do *Garlick*,
and other *Hautgouts* as nauſeous
altogether. In the mean time,

---

† *Of which ſome would have it a courſer ſort,*
inamœni odoris, *as the ſame Comedian names it
in his* Equites, *p.* 239. *and* 240. Edit. Baſil.
*See likewiſe this diſcuſs'd, together with its Pro-
perties, moſt copiouſly, in* Jo. Budæus *a* Stapul.
Comment. *in* Theophraſt. lib. vi. cap. 1. *and*
Bauhin. Hiſt. Plant. lib. xxvii. cap. 53.

Gar-

Garcius, *Bontius*, and others, af-
fure us, that the *Indians* at this
day univerfally fauce their Viands
with it ; and the *Bramin's* (who
eat no Flefh at all) inrich their
Sallets, by conftantly rubbing the
Difhes with it. Nor are fome of
our own skilful *Cooks* Ignorant,
how to condite and ufe it, with
the Applaufe of thofe, who, ignorant of the Secret, have admir'd
the richnefs of the Guft it has
imparted, when it has been fub-
ftituted inftead of all our *Cipol-
lati*, and other feafonings of that
Nature.

And thus have we done with
the various *Species* of all fuch
Efculents as may properly enter
the Compofition of our *Acetaria*,
and cold *Sallet*. And if I have
briefly touch'd upon their Na-
tures, Degrees, and *primary Qualities*, which *Intend* or *Remit*, as
to the Scale of *Heat*, *Cold*, *Drinefs*,
Moifture, &c. (which is to be un-
G   der-

derstood according to the different Texture of their *component Particles*) it has not been without what I thought necessary for the Instruction of the *Gatherer*, and *Sallet-Dresser*; how he ought to choose, sort, and mingle his Materials and Ingredients together.

What Care and Circumspection should attend the choice and collection of *Sallet* Herbs, has been partly shew'd. I can therefore, by no means, approve of that extravagant Fancy of some, who tell us, that a *Fool* is as fit to be the *Gatherer* of a *Sallet* as a *Wiser* Man. Because, say they, one can hardly choose amiss, provided the Plants be green, young, and tender, where-ever they meet with them: But sad experience shews, how many fatal Mistakes have been committed by those who took the deadly *Cicutæ*, *Hemlocks*, *Aconits*, &c. for Garden

den *Persley*, and *Parsneps*; the *Myrrhis Sylvestris*, or *Cow-Weed*, for *Chærophilum*, (*Chervil*) *Thapsia* for *Fennel*; the wild *Chondrilla* for *Succory*; *Dogs-Mercury* instead of *Spinach*: *Papaver Corniculatum Luteum*, and horn'd *Poppy* for *Eringo*; *Oenanthe aquatica* for the *Palustral Apium*, and a world more, whose dire effects have been many times sudden Death, and the cause of Mortal Accidents to those who have eaten of them unwittingly: But supposing some of those wild and unknown Plants should not prove so *deleterious* and * unwholsome; yet may others of them annoy the *Head*, *Brain*, and *Genus Nervosum*, weaken the *Eyes*, offend the *Stomach*, affect the *Liver*, torment the *Bowels*, and discover their malignity in

___

* Vide *Cardanum* de usu Cibi.

G 2   dange-

dangerous and dreadful *Symptoms.* And therefore such *Plants* as are rather *Medicinal* than *Nourishing* and *Refreshing*, are studiously to be rejected. So highly necessary it is, that what we sometimes find in *old Books* concerning *Edules* of other Countries and Climates (frequently call'd by the Names of such as are wholsome in ours, and among us) mislead not the unskilful Gatherer; to prevent which we read of divers *Popes* and *Emperors*, that had sometimes Learned *Physicians* for their *Master-Cooks.* I cannot therefore but exceedingly approve of that charitable Advice of Mr. *Ray* * (*Transact. Num.*238.) who thinks it the Interest of Mankind, that all Persons should be caution'd of advent'ring upon unknown Herbs and Plants to

---

* *Vol.* xx.

their

their Prejudice: Of ſuch, I ſay, with our excellent * *Poet* (a little chang'd)

Happy from ſuch conceal'd, if ſtill
do lie,
Of Roots and Herbs the unwholſome *Luxury.*

The Illuſtrious and Learned *Columna* has, by obſerving what † *Inſects* did uſually feed on, make Conjectures of the Nature of the Plants. But I ſhould not ſo readily adventure upon it on that account, as to its wholſomneſs: For tho' indeed one may ſafely eat of a *Peach* or *Abricot,* after a *Snail* has been Taſter, I queſtion whether it might be

---

* Cowley:

Ουδ' ὅσον ἐν μαλάχῃ τε κ᾽ ἀσφοδέλῳ μέγ'
ὄνειαρ
Κρύψαντες γὰρ ἔχυσι θεοὶ βίον ἀνθρώποισι.

Heſiod.

† *Concerning this of Inſects, See* Mr. Ray's *Hiſt. Plant.* li. 1. cap. 24.

G 3　　　　　　　　　ſo

ſo of all other Fruits and Herbs attack'd by other *Inſects:* Nor would one conclude, the *Hyoſcyamus* harmleſs, becauſe the *Cimex* feeds upon it, as the Learned Dr. *Lyſter* has diſcover'd. Notice ſhould therefore be taken what *Eggs* of *Inſects* are found adhering to the Leaves of *Sallet-Herbs*, and frequently cleave ſo firmly to them, as not eaſily to be waſh'd off, and ſo not being taken notice of, paſſing for accidental and harmleſs Spots only, may yet produce very ill effects.

Grillus, who according to the Doctrine of *Tranſmigration* (as *Plutarch* tells us) had, in his turn, been a *Beaſt* ; diſcourſes how much better he fed, and liv'd, than when he was turn'd to *Man* again, as knowing then, what Plants were beſt and moſt proper for him: Whilſt Men, *Sarcophagiſts* (Fleſh-Eaters) in all this time were yet to ſeek.

And

And 'tis indeed very evident, that Cattel, and other πάνφαγα, and *herbaceous* Animals which feed on Plants, are directed by their Smell, and accordingly make election of their Food: But Men (besides the *Smell* and *Taste*) have, or should have, *Reason, Experience*, and the Aids of *Natural Philosophy* to be their Guides in this Matter. We have heard of *Plants*, that (like the *Basilisk*) kill and infect by * looking on them only; and some by the touch. The truth is, there's need of all the Senses to determine *Analogically* concerning the Vertues and Properties, even of the *Leaves* alone of many *Edule-Plants*: The most

---

* *The poyson'd Weeds : I have seen a Man, who was so poyson'd with it, that the Skin peel'd off his Face, and yet he never touch'd it, only looked on it as he pass'd by.* Mr. Stafford, *Philos. Transact.* Vol. III. Num. xl. p. 794.

G 4 emi

eminent Principles of near the whole Tribe of *Sallet* Vegetables, inclining rather to *Acid* and *Sowre* than to any other quality, especially, Salt, Sweet, or Luscious. There is therefore Skill and Judgment requir'd, how to suit and mingle our *Sallet*-Ingredients, so as may best agree with the Constitution of the (vulgarly reputed) *Humors* of those who either stand in need of, or affect these Refreshments, and by so adjusting them, that as nothing should be suffer'd to domineer, so should none of them lose their genuine Gust, Savour, or Vertue. To this end,

The Cooler, and moderately refreshing, should be chosen to extinguish Thirst, attemper the Blood, repress Vapours, &c.

The Hot, Dry, Aromatic, Cordial and friendly to the Brain, may be qualify'd by the Cold and Moist: The Bitter and Stomachical

chical, with the *Sub-acid* and
gentler Herbs : The *Mordicant*
and pungent, and such as repress
or discuss Flatulency (revive
the Spirits, and aid Concoction;)
with such as abate, and take off
the keenness, mollify and recon-
cile the more harsh and churlish :
The mild and insipid, animated
with *piquant* and brisk : The
Astringent and Binders, with
such as are Laxative and Deob-
struct : The over-sluggish, raw,
and unactive, with those that
are *Eupeptic*, and promote Concoction : There are *Pectorals* for
the Breast and Bowels. Those of
middle Nature, according as they
appear to be more or less *Speci-
fic* ; and as their Characters (tho'
briefly) are describ'd in our foregoing *Catalogue :* For notwithstanding it seem in general, that
raw *Sallets* and *Herbs* have expe-
rimentally been found to be the
most soveraign Diet in that *Ende-
mial*

mial (and indeed with us, *Epidemical* and almost universal) Contagion the *Scorbute*, to which we of this Nation, and most other *Islanders* are obnoxious; yet, since the *Nasturtia* are singly, and alone as it were, the most effectual, and powerful Agents in conquering and expugning that cruel Enemy; it were enough to give the *Sallet-Dresser* direction how to choose, mingle, and proportion his Ingredients; as well as to shew what Remedies there are contain'd in our Magazine of *Sallet-Plant* upon all Occasions, rightly marshal'd and skilfully apply'd. So as (with our * sweet *Cowley*)

If thro the strong and beauteous Fence
Of Temperance and Innocence,
And wholsome Labours, and a quiet
  Diseases passage find; (*Mind,*

---

* Cowley, *Garden*, Miscel. Stanz. 8.

They

They muſt not think here to aſſail
A Land unarm'd, or without Guard,
They muſt fight for it, and diſpute
it hard,
Before they can prevail;
Scarce any Plant is uſed here,
Which 'gainſt ſome Aile a Weapon
does not bear.

We have ſaid how neceſſary it
is, that in the Compoſure of a
Sallet, every Plant ſhould come
in to bear its part, without being over-power'd by ſome Herb
of a ſtronger Taſte, ſo as to en-
danger the native *Sapor* and Vertue of the reſt; but fall into
their places, like the *Notes* in
Muſic, in which there ſhould be
nothing harſh or grating: And
tho admitting ſome *Diſcords* (to
diſtinguiſh and illuſtrate the reſt)
ſtriking in the more ſprightly, and
ſometimes gentler Notes, recon-
cile all Diſſonancies, and melt
them into an agreeable Compoſition.

ſition. Thus the Comical *Ma-
ſter-Cook*, introduc'd by *Damoxe-
nus*, when asked πῶς ἐςιν αὐτοῖς
συμφωνία; *What Harmony there
was in Meats?* The very ſame
(ſays he) that a *Diateſſaron, Di-
apente*, and *Diapaſon* have one to
another in a Conſort of Muſic:
And that there was as great care
requir'd, not to mingle * *Sapores*

---

* Sapores minime Conſentientes καὶ συμ-
πλεκομῄας ἐχὶ συμφώνυς ἀφᾶς: Hæc deſpi-
cere ingenioſi eſt artificis: *Neither did the Ar-
tiſt mingle his Proviſions without extraordinary
Study and Conſideration:* Ἀλλὰ μίξας πάνja
χατὰ συμφωνίαν. Horum ſingulis ſeorſum aſ-
ſumptis, tu expedito: Sic ego tanquam Ora-
culo jubeo.——Itaque literarum ignarum Co-
quum, tu cum videris, & qui Democriti ſcripta
omnia non perlegerit, vel potius, impromptu
non habeat, eum deride ut futilem: Ac il-
lum Mercede conducito, qui Epicuri Canonem
uſu plane didicerit, *&c. as it follows in the*
Gaſtronomia *of* Archeſtratus, Athen. lib. xxiii.
Such another BragadoccioCook Horace *deſcribes,*

Nec ſibiCœnarum quivis temerè arroget artem
Non prius exactâ tenui ratione ſaporem.

Sat. lib. ii. *Sat.* 4.

minime

minime consentientes, jarring and repugnant Tastes; looking upon him as a lamentable Ignorant, who should be no better vers'd in *Democritus.* The whole *Scene* is very diverting, as *Athenæus* presents it ; and to the same sense *Macrobius*, *Saturn. lib.* 1. *cap.* 1. In short, the main Skill of the Artist lies in this:

What choice to choose, for delicacy
   best ;
What Order so contriv'd, as not to
   mix
Tastes not well join'd, inelegant,
   but bring
Taste after Taste, upheld by kind-
   liest change.

As our * *Paradisian Bard* intro-
duces *Eve*, dressing of a *Sallet* for her *Angelical* Guest.

_____

* Milton's *Paradise Lost.*

       Thus

Thus, by the discreet choice and mixture of the *Oxoleon* (*Oyl, Vinegar, Salt,* &c.) the Composition is perfect; so as neither the *Prodigal, Niggard,* nor *Insipid,* should (according to the *Italian* Rule) prescribe in my Opinion; since *One* may be too profuse, the *Other* * over-saving, and the *Third* (like himself) give it no Relish at all: It may be too *sharp,* if it exceed a grateful *Acid* ; too *Insulse* and flat, if the Profusion be extream. From all which it appears, that a Wise-Man is the proper Composer of an excellent *Sallet,* and how many *Transcendences* belong to an accomplish'd *Sallet-Dresser* , so as to emerge an exact *Critic* indeed, He should be skill'd in the Degrees, Terms, and various *Species*

---

* Qui
Tingat olus siccum muria vafer in calice emptâ,
Ipse sacrum irrorans piper —— Perf. *Sat.* vi.

of

of *Tastes*, according to the *Scheme* set us down in the *Tables* of the Learned * Dr. *Grew*, to which I refer the Curious.

'Tis moreover to be consider'd, that *Edule* Plants are not in all their Tastes and Vertues alike: For as Providence has made us to consist of different Parts and Members, both Internal and External; so require they different Juices to nourish and supply them: Wherefore the force and activity of some Plants lie in the *Root*; and even the *Leaves* of some *Bitter-Roots* are sweet, and *è contra*. Of others, in the *Stem*, *Leaves*, *Buds*, *Flowers*, &c. Some exert their Vigour without *Decoction*; others being a little press'd or contus'd; others again *Raw*, and best in Consort; some alone, and *per se* without

---

Dr. Grew, Lect. vi. c. 2, 3.

any

any σκευασία, Preparation, or
Mixture at all. Care therefore
muſt be taken by the *Collector*,
that what he gathers anſwer to
theſe Qualities; and that as near
as he can, they conſiſt (I ſpeak
of the *cruder Salleting*) of the
Oluſcula, and *ex foliis pubeſcenti-
bus*, or (as *Martial* calls them)
Prototomi rudes, and very tendereſt Parts *Gems*, young *Buds*,
and even firſt Rudiments of their
ſeveral Plants; ſuch as we ſometimes find in the *Craws* of the
Wood-Culver, *Stock-Dove*, *Par-
tridge*, *Pheaſants*, and other Up-
land Fowl, where we have a natural *Sallet*, pick'd, and almoſt
dreſs'd to our hands.

I. Preparatory to the Dreſſing
therefore, let your Herby Ingredients be exquiſitely cull'd, and
cleans'd of all worm-eaten, ſlimy,
canker'd, dry, ſpotted, or any ways
vitiated Leaves. And then that
they

they be rather difcreetly fprinkl'd, than over-much fob'd with Spring-Water, efpecially *Lettuce*, which Dr. * *Muffet* thinks impairs their Vertue; but this, I fuppofe he means of the *Cabbage*-kind, whofe heads are fufficiently protected by the outer Leaves which cover it. After wafhing, let them remain a while in the *Cullenaer*, to drain the fuperfluous moifture: And laftly, fwing them altogether gently in a clean courfe Napkin; and fo they will be in perfect condition to receive the *Intinctus* following.

II. That the *Oyl*, an Ingredient fo indifpenfibly and highly neceffary, as to have obtain'd the name of *Cibarium* (and with us of *Sallet-Oyl*) be very clean, not high-colour'd, nor yellow; but

---

* *Muffet*, de Diæta, *c.* 23.

H   with

with an Eye rather of a pallid *Olive* green, without Smell, or the least touch of *rancid*, or indeed of any other sensible Taste or Scent at all ; but smooth, light, and pleasant upon the Tongue ; such as the genuine *Omphacine*, and native *Luca Olives* afford, fit to allay the tartness of *Vinegar*, and other *Acids*, yet gently to warm and humectate where it passes. Some who have an aversion to *Oyl*, substitute fresh *Butter* in its stead ; but 'tis so exceedingly clogging to the Stomach, as by no means to be allow d.

III. *Thirdly*, That the *Vinegar*, and other liquid *Acids*, perfectly clear, neither sowre, *Vapid* or spent ; be of the best Wine Vinegar, whether Distill'd, or otherwise *Aromatiz'd*, and impregnated with the Infusion of *Clovegillyflowers*, *Elder*, *Roses*, *Rosemary*,

mary, *Nasturtium*, &c. inrich'd with the Vertues of the Plant.

A *Verjuice* not unfit for *Sallet*, is made by a *Grape* of that Name, or the green immature Clusters of most other Grapes, press'd, and put into a small Vessel to ferment.

IV. *Fourthly*, That the *Salt* (*aliorum Condimentorum Condimentum*, as *Plutarch* calls it) detersive, penetrating, quickning (and so great a resister of Putrefaction, and universal use, as to have sometimes merited Divine Epithets) be of the brightest *Bay grey-Salt* ; moderately dried, and *contus'd*, as being the least Corrosive : But of this, as of *Sugar* also, which some mingle with the *Salt* (as warming without heating) if perfectly refin'd, there would be no great difficulty ; provided none, save Ladies, were of the Mess ; whilst

the

the perfection of *Sallets*, and
that which gives them the name,
consists in the grateful *Saline A-
cid*-point, temper'd as is directed, and which we find to be most
esteem'd by judicious Palates :
Some, in the mean time, have
been so nice, and luxuriously curious as for the heightning, and
(as they affect to speak) giving
the utmost *poinant* and *Relevèe*
in lieu of our vulgar *Salt*, to recommend and cry-up the *Essen-
tial-Salts* and *Spirits* of the most
Sanative Vegetables; or such of
the *Alcalizate* and *Fixt*; extract-
ed from the *Calcination* of *Baulm,
Rosemary, Wormwood, Scurvy-
grass*, &c. Affirming that without
the gross Plant, we might have
healing, cooling, generous, and
refreshing *Cordials*, and all the
Materia Medica out of the *Salt-
Cellar* only : But to say no more
of this Impertinence, as to *Salts*
of *Vegetables*; many indeed there
be,

be, who reckon them not much
unlike in Operation, however
different in *Taste*, *Crystals*, and
Figure: It being a question, whether they at all retain the Vertues and Faculties of their *Simples.* unless they could be made
without *Colcination.* *Franciscus
Redi*, gives us his Opinion of
this, in a *Process* how they are
to be prepar'd ; and so does our
Learned * Doctor (whom we
lately nam'd) whether *Lixivial*,
Essential, *Marine*, or other facti-
tious *Salts* of Plants, with their
Qualities, and how they differ :
But since 'tis thought all *Fixed
Salts* made the *common way*, are
little better than our *common Salt*,
let it suffice, that our *Sallet-Salt*
be of the best ordinary *Bay-Salt*,

---

* *Dr.* Grew, *Annat. Plant.* Lib. 1. Sect. iv.
cap. 1, *&c.* See also, Transact. Num. 107.
Vol. ix.

clean, bright, dry, and without clamminess.

Of *Sugar* (by some call'd *Indian-Salt*) as it is rarely us'd in *Sallet*, it should be of the best refined, white, hard, close, yet light and sweet as the *Madera*'s: Nourishing, preserving, cleansing, delighting the Taste, and preferrable to *Honey* for most uses. *Note*, That both *this*, *Salt*, and *Vinegar*, are to be proportion'd to the Constitution, as well as what is said of the Plants themselves. The one for cold, the other for hot Stomachs.

V. That the *Mustard* (another noble Ingredient) be of the best *Tewksberry*; or else compos'd of the soundest and weightiest *Yorkshire Seed*, exquisitely sifted, winnow'd, and freed from the Husks, a little (not over-much) dry'd by the Fire, temper'd to the consistence of a Pap with *Vinegar*, in

in which shavings of the *Horse
Radish* have been steep'd : Then
cutting an *Onion*, and putting it
into a small Earthen *Gally-Pot*,
or some thick *Glass* of that shape;
pour the *Mustard* over it, and
close it very well with a *Cork*.
There be, who preserve the
Flower and Dust of the bruised
Seed in a well-stopp'd Glass, to
temper, and have it fresh when
they please. But what is yet by
some esteem'd beyond all these,
is compos'd of the dried Seeds of
the *Indian Nasturtium*, reduc'd
to Powder, finely bolted, and
mixt with a little *Levain*, and so
from time to time made fresh, as
indeed all other *Mustard* should
be.

Note, That the Seeds are
pounded in a Mortar ; or bruis'd
with a polish'd *Cannon-Bullet*, in
a large wooden Bowl-Dish, or
which is most preferr'd, ground
H 4   in

in a *Quern* contriv'd for this purpose only.

VI. *Sixthly,* That the *Pepper* (white or black) be not bruis'd to too small a Dust; which, as we caution'd, is very prejudicial. And here let me mention the *Root* of the *Minor Pimpinella,* or small *Burnet Saxifrage* ; which being dried, is by some extoll'd beyond all other *Peppers,* and more wholsom.

Of other *Strewings* and *Aromatizers,* which may likewise be admitted to inrich our *Sallet,* we have already spoken, where we mention *Orange* and *Limonpeel* ; to which may also be added, *Jamaica-Pepper, Juniper-berries,* &c. as of singular Vertue.

Nor here should I omit (the mentioning at least of) *Saffron,* which the *German* Housewives have a way of forming into Balls,

Balls, by mingling it with a little *Honey*; which throughly dried, they reduce to Powder, and sprinkle it over their *Sallets* for a noble *Cordial.* Those of *Spain* and *Italy*, we know, generally make use of this Flower, mingling its golden Tincture with almost every thing they eat; But its being so apt to prevail above every thing with which 'tis blended, we little incourage its admittance into our *Sallet*.

VII. Seventhly, That there be the Yolks of fresh and new-laid *Eggs*, boil'd moderately hard, to be mingl'd and mash'd with the *Mustard*, *Oyl*, and *Vinegar*; and part to cut into quarters, and eat with the Herbs.

VIII. *Eighthly*, (according to the *super*-curious) that the *Knife*, with which the *Sallet Herbs* are cut (especially *Oranges*, *Limons*, &c.)

be

he of *Silver*, and by no means of *Steel*, which all *Acids* are apt to corrode, and retain a Metalic relish of.

IX. *Ninthly* and *Lastly*, That the *Saladiere*, (Sallet-Dishes) be of *Porcelane*, or of the *Holland-Delft-Ware* ; neither too deep nor shallow , according to the quantity of the *Sallet* Ingredients ; *Pewter*, or even *Silver*, not at all so well agreeing with *Oyl* and *Vinegar*, which leave their several Tinctures. And note, That there ought to be one of the Dishes, in which to beat and mingle the Liquid *Vehicles* ; and a second to receive the crude Herbs in, upon which they are to be pour'd ; and then with a Fork and a Spoon kept continually stirr'd , 'till all the Furniture be equally moisten'd : Some , who are Husbands of their *Oyl*, pour at first the *Oyl* alone,

alone, as more apt to commu-
nicate and diffuse its Slipperi-
ness, than when it is mingled
and beaten with the *Acids* ;
which they pour on last of all ;
and 'tis incredible how small
a quantity of *Oyl* (in this
quality, like the gilding of
Wyer) is sufficient, to imbue
a very plentiful assembly of
Sallet-Herbs.

The *Sallet-Gatherer* likewise
should be provided with a light,
and neatly made *Withy-Dutch-
Basket* , divided into several
Partitions.

Thus Instructed and knowing
in the *Apparatus* ; the *Species,
Proportions* , and manner of
Dressing, according to the several Seasons you have in the
following Table.

It

It being one of the Inquiries of the Noble * Mr. *Boyle,* what *Herbs* were proper and fit to make *Sallets* with, and how beſt to order them? we have here (by the Aſſiſtance of Mr. *London,* His Majeſty's Principal Gard'ner) reduc'd them to a competent Number, not exceeding *Thirty Five* ; but which may be vary'd and inlarg'd, by taking-in, or leaving out, any other *Sallet*-Plant, mention'd in the foregoing Liſt, under theſe three or four Heads.

---

* *Philoſoph. Tranſact.* Vol. III. Num. xl. p. 799.

I. *Species.*

But all these sorts are not to be had at the very same time, and therefore we have divided them into the *Quarterly Seasons*, each containing and lasting Three Months.

Note, That by *Parts* is to be understood a *Pugil*; which is no more than one does usually take up between the Thumb and the two next Fingers. By *Fascicule* a reasonable full Grip, or Handful.

Farther

Farther Directions concerning the proper Seasons, *for the* Gathering, Composing, *and* Dressing *of a* Sallet.

AND *First*, as to the *Season*, both *Plants* and *Roots* are then properly to be *Gather'd*, and in prime, when most they abound with Juice and in Vigour: Some in the *Spring*, or a little anticipating it before they Blossom, or are in full Flower: Some in the *Autumnal* Months; which later Season many preferr, the Sap of the Herb, tho' not in such exuberance, yet as being then better concocted, and so render'd fit for *Salleting*, 'till the Spring begins a fresh to put forth new, and tender Shoots and Leaves.

This,

This, indeed, as to the *Root*, newly taken out of the Ground is true; and therefore should such have their *Germination* stopt the sooner: The approaching and prevailing Cold, both Maturing and Impregnating them; as does Heat the contrary, which now would but exhaust them: But for those other *Esculents* and Herbs imploy'd in our *Composition* of *Sallets*, the early *Spring*, and ensuing Months (till they begin to mount, and prepare to *Seed*) is certainly the most natural, and kindly Season to collect and accommodate them for the Table. Let none then consult *Culpeper*, or the *Figure flingers*, to inform them when the governing *Planet* is in its *Exaltation*; but look upon the *Plants* themselves, and judge of their Vertues by their own Complexions.

More-

Moreover, In *Gathering*, Respect is to be had to their Proportions, as provided for in the *Table* under that Head, be the Quality whatsoever: For tho' there is indeed nothing more wholsome than *Lettuce* and *Mustard* for the *Head* and *Eyes*; yet either of them eaten in excess, were highly prejudicial to them both: Too much of the *first* extreamly debilitating and weakning the *Ventricle*, and hastning the further decay of sickly *Teeth*; and of the *second* the *Optic Nerves*, and *Sight* it self; the like may be said of all the rest. I conceive therefore, a Prudent Person, well acquainted with the Nature and Properties of *Sallet-Herbs*, &c. to be both the fittest *Gatherer* and *Composer* too; which yet will require no great Cunning, after once he is acquainted with our *Table* and *Catalogue*.

We

We purposely, and *in transitu* only, take notice here of the Pickl'd, *Muriated*, or otherwise prepared Herbs ; excepting some such Plants, and Proportions of them, as are of hard digestion, and not fit to be eaten altogether *Crude*, (of which in the *Appendix*) and among which I reckon *Ash-keys*, *Broom-buds* and *Pods*, *Haricos*, *Gurkems*, *Olives*, *Capers*, the Buds and Seeds of *Nasturtia*, *Young Wall-nuts*, *Pineapples*, *Eringo*, *Cherries*, *Cornelians*, *Berberries*, &c. together with several Stalks, Roots, and Fruits ; Ordinary Pot-herbs, *Anis*, *Cistus Hortorum*, *Horminum*, *Pulegium*, *Satureia*, *Thyme* ; the intire Family of Pulse and *Legumena* ; or other *Sauces*, *Pies*, *Tarts*, *Omlets*, *Tansie*, *Farces*, &c. *Condites* and Preserves with *Sugar* by the Hand of Ladies ; tho' they are all of them the genuine Production of the *Garden*, and mention'd in

I   our

our *Kalendar*, together with their Culture; whilst we confine our selves to such Plants and *Esculenta* as we find at hand; delight our selves to gather, and are easily prepar'd for an *Extemporary Collation*, or to Usher in, and Accompany other (more Solid, tho' haply not more Agreeable) Dishes, as the Custom is.

But there now starts up a Question, Whether it were better, or more proper, to *Begin* with *Sallets*, or *End* and Conclude with them? Some think the harder Meats should first be eaten for better Concoction; others, those of easiest Digestion, to make way, and prevent Obstruction; and this makes for our *Sallets*, *Horarii*, and *Fugaces Fructus* (as they call 'em) to be eaten first of all, as agreeable to the general Opinion of the great *Hippocrates*, and *Galen*, and of *Celsus* before him. And therefore the *French*
do

do well, to begin with their *Herbaceous Pottage*, and for the *Cruder*, a Reason is given:

* *Prima tibi dabitur Ventri* Lactuca *movendo*
Utilis, & Poris fila resecta suis.

And tho' this Custom came in about *Domitian*'s time †, ὁ μ̄ ἀρχαῖοι, they anciently did quite the contrary,

‖ *Gratáque nobilium Lactuca ciborum.*

But of later Times, they were constant at the *Ante-cœnia*, eating plentifully of *Sallet*, especially of *Lettuce*, and more refrigerating Herbs. Nor without

---

* Mart. *Epig. lib.* xi. 39.
† Athen. l. 2. *Of which Change of Diet see* Plut. iv. *Sympos.* 9. Plinii *Epist.* 1. *ad Eretrium.*
‖ Virg. *Moreto.*

Cause :

Cause : For drinking liberally, they were found to expell, and allay the Fumes and Vapors of the *genial Compotation*, the spirituous Liquor gently conciliating Sleep : Besides, that being of a crude nature, more dispos'd, and apt to fluctuate, corrupt, and disturb a surcharg'd Stomach ; they thought convenient to begin with *Sallets*, and innovate the ancient Usage.

* —— *Nam Lactuca innatat acri Post Vinum Stomacho*——

For if on drinking Wine you Lettuce eat,
It floats upon the Stomach ——

The *Spaniards*, notwithstanding, eat but sparingly of Herbs at Dinner, especially *Lettuce*, beginning with *Fruit*, even before

---

* Hor. *Sat. l.* 2. *Sat.* 4.

the

the *Olio* and Hot-Meats come to the Table; drinking their Wine pure, and eating the beft Bread in the World; fo as it feems the Queftion ftill remains undecided with them,

† *Claudere quæ cænas* Lactuca *fo-
    lebat avorum
    Dic mihi cur noftras inchoat
    illa dapes?*

The *Sallet,* which of old came in
    at laft,
Why now with it begin we our
    Repaft?

And now fince we mention'd *Fruit,* there rifes another Scruple: Whether *Apples, Pears, Abricots, Cherries, Plums,* and other Tree, and *Ort-yard-Fruit,* are to be reckon'd among *Salleting;* and when likewife moft

---

† Mart. *Ep. l.* v. *Ep.* 17.

I 3

feaseasonably to be eaten? But as none of these do properly belong to our *Catalogue* of *Herbs* and *Plants*, to which this Discourse is confin'd (besides what we may occasionally speak of hereafter) there is a very useful * Treatise on that Subject already publish'd. We hasten then in the next place to the *Dressing*, and *Composing* of our *Sallet:* For by this time, our Scholar may long to see the *Rules* reduc'd to *Practice*, and Refresh himself with what he finds growing among his own *Lactuceta* and other Beds of the *Kitchin-Garden.*

---

* *Concerning the Use of Fruit (besides many others) whether best to be eaten before, or after Meals? Published by a Physician of* Rochel, *and render'd out of* French *into* English. *Printed by* T. Basset *in* Fleetstreet.

DRES-

DRESSING.

I Am not ambitious of being thought an excellent *Cook*, or of those who set up, and value themselves, for their Skill in *Sauces* ; such as was *Mithacus* a *Culinary Philosopher* , and other *Eruditæ Gulæ* ; who read Lectures of *Hautgouts*, like the *Archestratus* in *Athenæus :* Tho' after what we find the *Heroes* did of old , and see them chining out the slaughter'd *Ox*, dressing the Meat, and do the Offices of both *Cook* and *Butcher*, (for so * *Homer* represents *Achilles* himself, and the rest of those Illustrious *Greeks*) I say, after this, let none reproach our *Sallet-Dresser*, or disdain so clean, innocent, sweet,

---

* Achilles, Patroclus, Automedon. *Iliad.*ix. *& alibi.*

and

and Natural a Quality ; compar'd with the Shambles Filth and *Nidor*, Blood and Cruelty ; whilst all the World were *Eaters*, and *Composers* of *Sallets* in its best and brightest Age.

The Ingredients therefore gather'd and proportion'd, as above ; Let the *Endive* have all its out-side Leaves stripp'd off, slicing *in* the White: In like manner the *Sellery* is also to have the hollow green Stem or Stalk trimm'd and divided ; slicing-in the blanched Part, and cutting the Root into four equal Parts.

Lettuce, *Cresses*, *Radish*, &c. (as was directed) must be exquisitely pick'd, cleans'd, wash'd, and put into the Strainer ; swing'd, and shaken gently, and, if you please, separately, or all together ; Because some like not so well the *Blanch'd* and Bitter Herbs, if eaten with the rest : Others mingle
Endive,

Endive, *Succory,* and *Rampions,*
without diſtinction, and generally eat *Sellery* by it ſelf, as alſo
Sweet *Fennel.*

From *April* till *September* (and
during all the Hot *Months*) may
Guinny-Pepper, and *Horſe-Radiſh*
be left out; and therefore we
only mention them in the Dreſſing, which ſhould be in this
manner.

Your *Herbs* being handſomly
parcell'd, and ſpread on a clean
Napkin before you, are to be
mingl'd together in one of the
Earthen glaz'd Diſhes: Then,
for the *Oxoleon* ; Take of clear,
and perfectly good *Oyl-Olive,*
three Parts; of ſharpeſt *Vinegar*
(‖ ſweeteſt of all *Condiments*)
Limon, or Juice of *Orange,* one

‖ *For ſo ſome pronounce it,* V. Athenæum
Deip. Lib. II. *Cap.* 26. ἡδ⊙ quaſi ἡδύσμα,
*perhaps for that it incites Appetite, and cauſes
Hunger, which is the beſt Sauce.*

Part ;

Part ; and therein let steep some
Slices of *Horse-Radish*, with a
little *Salt :* Some in a separate
Vinegar, gently bruise a *Pod* of
Guinny-Pepper, straining both the
Vinegars apart, to make Use of
Either, or One alone, or of both,
as they best like ; then add as
much *Tewkesbury*, or other dry
Mustard grated, as will lie upon
an Half-Crown Piece : Beat, and
mingle all these very well together ; but pour not on the *Oyl*
and *Vinegar*, 'till immediately before the *Sallet* is ready to be eat-
en: And then with the *Yolk* of
two new-laid *Eggs* (boyl'd and
prepar'd, as before is taught)
squash, and bruise them all into
mash with a Spoon ; and lastly,
pour it all upon the *Herbs*, stirring, and mingling them 'till they
are well and throughly imbib'd ;
not forgetting the Sprinklings of
Aromaticks, and such Flowers, as
we have already mentioned, if
you

you think fit, and garnishing the
Dish with the thin Slices of *Horse-
Radish*, *Red Beet*, *Berberries*, &c.

Note, That the *Liquids* may
be made more, or less *Acid*, as is
most agreeable to your Taste.

> These *Rules*, and *Prescriptions*
> duly *Observ'd* ; you have a
> *Sallet* (for a Table of Six or
> Eight Persons) *Dress'd*, and
> Accommodated *secundum
> Artem* : For, as the † Pro-
> verb has it,

Ὀυ παντὸς ἀνδρὸς ἐςὶν ἀρτῦσαι
κᾳλῶς.
Non est cujusvis rectè condire.

AND now after all we have
advanc'd in favour of the *Herbaceous* Diet, there still emerges
a third Inquiry ; namely, Whether the Use of *Crude Herbs* and

---

† Cratinus in Glauco.

Plants are fo wholefom as is pretended?

What Opinion the Prince of Phyficians had of them, we fhall fee hereafter; as alfo what the Sacred Records of elder Times feem to infer, before there were any Flefh-Shambles in the World; together with the Reports of fuch as are often converfant among many Nations and People, who to this Day, living on *Herbs* and *Roots*, arrive to incredible Age, in conftant Health and Vigour: Which, whether attributable to the *Air* and *Climate*, *Cuftom*, *Conftitution*, &c. fhould be inquir'd into; efpecially, when we compare the *Antediluvians* mention'd *Gen.* 1.29.—the whole *Fifth* and *Ninth* Chapters, *ver.* 3. confining them to *Fruit* and wholefom *Sallets:* I deny not that both the *Air* and *Earth* might then be lefs humid and clammy, and confequently Plants, and

and Herbs better fermented, concocted, and less Rheumatick, than
since, and presently after; to say
nothing of the infinite Numbers
of putrid Carcasses of Dead A-
nimals, perishing in the Flood,
(of which I find few, if any, have
taken notice) which needs must
have corrupted the Air: Those
who live in Marshes, and Uliginous Places (like the Hundreds
of *Essex*) being more obnoxious
to *Fevers*, *Agues*, *Pleurisies*, and
generally unhealthful: The Earth
also then a very Bog, compar'd
with what it likely was before
that destructive *Cataclism*, when
Men breath'd the pure *Paradisian*
Air, sucking in a more *æthereal*,
nourishing, and baulmy *Pabulum*,
so foully vitiated now, thro' the
Intemperance, Luxury, and softer
Education and Effeminacy of the
Ages since.

   Custom, and *Constitution* come
next to be examin'd, together
with

with the Qualities, and *Vertue* of
the Food ; and I confeſs, the two
firſt, eſpecially that of *Conſtitution*, ſeems to me the more likely
Cauſe of Health, and conſequently of Long-life ; which induc'd
me to conſider of what Quality the uſual *Sallet* Furniture did
more eminently conſiſt, that ſo
it might become more ſafely ap-
plicable to the Temper, Humour,
and Diſpoſition of our Bodies ;
according to which, the various
Mixtures might be regulated and
proportion'd : There's no doubt,
but thoſe whoſe Conſtitutions
are Cold and Moiſt, are naturally affected with Things which
are Hot and Dry ; as on the
contrary, Hot, and Dry Complexions, with ſuch as cool and
refrigerate ; which perhaps made
the *Junior Gordian* (and others
like him) prefer the *frigidæ Men-
ſæ* (as of old they call'd *Sallets*)
which, according to *Cornelius
Celſus*,

Celfus, is the fitteſt Diet for *Obeſe*
and Corpulent Perſons, as not ſo
Nutritive, and apt to Pamper:
And conſequently, that for the
Cold, Lean, and Emaciated;
ſuch Herby Ingredients ſhould
be made choice of, as warm, and
cheriſh the Natural Heat, de-
pure the Blood, breed a laudable
Juice, and revive the Spirits:
And therefore my *Lord* * *Bacon*
ſhews what are beſt Raw, what
Boil'd, and what Parts of Plants
fitteſt to nouriſh. *Galen* indeed
ſeems to exclude them all, un-
leſs well accompanied with their
due Correctives, of which we
have taken care: Notwithſtanding yet, that even the moſt *Crude*
and *Herby*, actually Cold and
Weak, may potentially be Hot,

---

* Nat. Hiſt. IV. *Cent.* VII. 130. Se Ariſt.
Prob. *Sect.* xx. *Quæſt.* 36. *Why ſome Fruits and
Plants are beſt raw, others boil'd, roaſted, &c,
as becoming ſweeter; but the Crude more ſapid
and grateful.*

and

and Strengthning, as we find in
the moſt vigorous Animals, whoſe
Food is only Graſs. 'Tis true indeed, Nature has providentially
mingl'd, and dreſs'd a *Sallet* for
them in every Field, beſides
what they diſtinguiſh by Smell;
nor queſtion I, but Man at firſt
knew what Plants and Fruits
were good, before the Fall, by
his Natural Sagacity, and not
Experience; which ſince by Art,
and Trial, and long Obſervation
of their Properties and Effects,
they hardly recover: But in all
Events, ſuppoſing with * *Cardan*,
that Plants nouriſh little, they
hurt as little. Nay, Experience
tells us, that they not only hurt
not at all, but exceedingly benefit thoſe who uſe them; in-
du'd as they are with ſuch admirable Properties as they every

---

* Card. *Contradicent*. Med. l. iv. *Cant.* 18.
Diphilus *not at all*. Athenæus.

day

day difcover: For fome Plants
not only nourifh laudably, but
induce a manifeft and wholefom
Change ; as *Onions, Garlick, Rochet,* &c. which are both nutritive and warm ; *Lettuce, Purfe-
lan,* the *Intybs,* &c. and indeed
moft of the *Olera,* refrefh and
cool : And as their refpective
Juices being converted into the
Subftances of our Bodies, they become *Aliment* ; fo in regard of
their Change and Alteration, we
may allow them *Medicinal* ; efpecially the greater Numbers, a-
mong which we all this while have
skill but of very few (not only
in the Vegetable Kingdom, but
in the whole *Materia Medica*)
which may be juftly call'd *In-
fallible Specifics,* and upon whofe
Performance we may as fafely
depend, as we may on fuch as
familiarly we ufe for a **Crude**
Herb-Sallet ; difcreetly chofen,
mingl'd, and drefs'd accordingly:

K   Not

Not but that many of them may be improv'd, and render'd better in Broths, and Deco&ctions, than in *Oyl*, *Vinegar*, and other Liquids and Ingredients : But as this holds not in all, nay, perhaps in few comparatively, (provided, as I said, the Choice, Mixture, Conftitution, and *Seafon* rightly be underftood) we ftand up in Defence and Vindication of our *Sallet*, againft all Attacks and Oppofers whoever.

We have mentioned *Seafon*, and with the great *Hippocrates*, pronounce them more proper for the Summer, than the Winter ; and when thofe Parts of Plants us'd in *Sallet* are yet tender, delicate, and impregnated with the Vertue of the Spring, to cool, refrefh, and allay the Heat and Drought of the Hot and *Bilious*, Young and over-*Sanguine*, Cold, *Pituit*, and Melancholy ; in a word, for Perfons sons of all Ages, Humours, and Constitutions whatsoever.

To this of the *Annual Seasons,* we add that of *Culture* also, as of very great Importance: And this is often discover'd in the Taste, and consequently, in the Goodness of such Plants and *Salleting,* as are Rais'd and brought us fresh out of the Country, compar'd with those which the Avarice of the *Gardiner*, or Luxury rather of the Age, tempts them to force and *Resuscitate* of the most desirable and delicious Plants.

It is certain, says a * Learned Person, that about populous Cities, where Grounds are overforc'd for Fruit and early *Salleting*, nothing is more unwholsom: Men in the Country look so much more healthy and fresh;

---

* *Sir* Tho. Brown's *Miscel.*

K 2 and

and commonly are longer liv'd
than those who dwell in the
Middle and Skirts of vast and
crowded Cities, inviron'd with
rotten Dung, loathsome and
common Lay-Stalls; whose noi-
some Steams, wafted by the
Wind, poison and infect the
ambient Air and vital Spirits,
with those pernicious Exhalations,
and Materials of which they
make the *Hot Beds* for the raising those *Præcoces* indeed, and
forward Plants and Roots for
the wanton Palate; but which
being corrupt in the Original,
cannot but produce malignant
and ill Effects to those who feed
upon them. And the same was
well observ'd by the *Editor* of
our famous *Roger Bacon*'s Treatise concerning the *Cure of Old
Age*, and *Preservation of Youth*:
There being nothing so proper for
Sallet Herbs and other *Edule Plants*,
as the Genial and Natural Mould,
im-

impregnate, and enrich'd with well digested Compost (when requisite) without any Mixture of Garbage, odious Carrion, and other filthy Ordure, not half consum'd and ventilated and indeed reduc'd to the next Disposition of Earth it self, as it should be; and that in Sweet, || Rising, Aery and moderately Perflatile Grounds; where not only *Plants* but *Men* do last, and live much longer. Nor doubt I, but that every body would prefer Corn, and other Grain rais'd from *Marle, Chalk, Lime,* and other sweet Soil and Amendments, before that which is produc'd from the *Dunghil* only Beside, Experience shews, that the Rankness of *Dung* is frequently the Cause of Blasts and Smuttiness; as if the *Lord* of the *Universe,* by an

---

|| Caule suburbano qui siccis crevit in agris
Dulcior.———— Hor. *Sat.* l. 2. §. 4.

Act

Act of visible Providence would
check us, to take heed of all nn-
natural Sordidneſs and Mixtures.
We ſenſibly find this Difference
in Cattle and their Paſture ; but
moſt powerfully in *Fowl*, from
ſuch as are nouriſh'd with Corn,
ſweet and dry Food : And as of
Vegetable *Meats*, ſo of *Drinks*,
'tis obſerv'd, that the ſame Vine,
according to the Soil, produces a
Wine twice as heady as in the
ſame, and a leſs forc'd Ground ;
and the like I believe of all o-
ther Fruit, not to determine a-
ny thing of the *Peach* ſaid to be
Poiſon in *Perſia* ; becauſe 'tis a
Vulgar Error.

Now, becauſe among other
things, nothing more betrays its
unclean and ſpurious Birth than
what is ſo impatiently longed after as *Early Aſparagus*, &c. * Dr.
Liſter, (according to his commu-

---

* Tranſact. Philoſ. *Num.* xxv.

nicative

nicative and obliging Nature)
has taught us how to raise such as
our *Gardiners* cover with nasty
Litter, during the Winter; by
rather laying of Clean and Sweet
Wheat-Straw upon the Beds, *su-
per-seminating* and over-strowing
them thick with the Powder of
bruised *Oyster-Shells*, &c. to produce that most tender and delicious *Sallet*. In the mean while,
if nothing will satisfie save what
is rais'd *Ex tempore*, and by Mi-
racles of Art so long before the
time; let them study (like the
Adepti) as did a very ingenious
Gentleman whom I knew; That
having some Friends of his acci-
dentally come to Dine with
him, and wanting an early Sallet,
Before they sate down to Table,
sowed *Lettuce* and some other
Seeds in a certain Composition of
Mould he had prepared; which
within the space of two Hours,
being risen near two Inches high,

K 4　　　　　pre-

presented them with a delicate and tender *Sallet*; and this, without making use of any nauseous or fulsome Mixture; but of Ingredients not altogether so cheap perhaps. *Honoratus Faber* (no mean *Philosopher*) shews us another Method by sowing the Seeds steep'd in *Vinegar*, casting on it a good Quantity of *Bean-Shell* Ashes, irrigating them with *Spirit of Wine*, and keeping the Beds well cover'd under dry Matts. Such another Process for the raising early *Peas* and *Beans*, &c. we have the like * Accounts of: But were they practicable and certain, I confess I should not be fonder of them, than of such as the honest industrious Country-man's Field, and Good-Wife's Garden seasonably produce; where they are legitimately born in just

---

* *Num.* xviii.

time,

time, and without forcing Nature.

But to return again to *Health* and *Long Life*, and the Wholesomneſs of the Herby-Diet, * *John Beverovicius*, a Learn'd Phyſician (out of *Peter Moxa*, a *Spaniard*) treating of the extream Age, which thoſe of *America* uſually arrive to, aſſerts in behalf of Crude and Natural Herbs : *Diphilus* of old, as † *Athenæus* tells us, was on the other ſide, againſt all the Tribe of *Olera* in general ; and *Cardan* of late (as already noted) no great Friend to them ; Affirming Fleſh-Eaters to be much wiſer and more ſagacious. But this his ‖ Learned Antagoniſt utterly denies ; Whole Nations, Fleſh-Devourers (ſuch as the fartheſt *Northern*) becoming Heavy,

---

* *Theſaur. Sanit.* c. 2.
† *As* Delcampius *interprets the Place.*
‖ Scaliger *ad* Card. Exercit. 213.

Dull,

Dull, Unactive, and much more Stupid than the *Southern* ; and such as feed much on Plants, are more Acute, Subtil, and of deeper Penetration : Witneſs the *Chaldæans*, *Aſſyrians*, *Ægyptians*, &c. And further argues from the ſhort Lives of moſt *Carnivorous* Animals, compared with Graſs Feeders, and the Ruminating kind ; as the *Hart*, *Camel*, and the longævous *Elephant*, and other Feeders on Roots and Vegetables.

I know what is pretended of our Bodies being compoſed of *Diſſimilar* Parts, and ſo requiring Variety of Food : Nor do I reject the Opinion, keeping to the ſame *Species* ; of which there is infinitely more Variety in the *Herby* Family, than in all Nature beſides : But the Danger is in the *Generical* Difference of *Fleſh*, *Fiſh*, *Fruit*, &c. with other made Diſhes and exotic Sauces ; which a wanton and expenſive Luxury

has

has introduc'd ; debauching the
Stomach, and sharpening it to
devour things of such difficult
Concoction, with those of more
easie Digestion, and of contrary
Substances, more than it can well
dispose of : Otherwise Food of
the same kind would do us little
hurt : So true is that of * *Celsus*,
*Eduntur facilius ; ad concoctionem
autem materiæ, genus, & modus
pertineat.* They are (says he)
easily eaten and taken in : But
regard should be had to their Digestion, Nature, Quantity and
Quality of the Matter. As to
that of *Dissimilar* Parts, requiring this contended-for Variety :
If we may judge by other Animals (as I know not why we may
not) there is (after all the late
Contests about *Comparative Ana-
tomy*) so little Difference in the

---

* *Cel.* Lib. Cap. 4.

Stru-

Structure, as to the Use of those Parts and Vessels destin'd to serve the Offices of Concoction, Nutrition, and other Separations for Supply of Life, &c. That it does not appear why there should need any Difference at all of Food; of which the most simple has ever been esteem'd the best, and most wholsome; according to that of the † Naturalist, *Hominis cibus utilissimus simplex*. And that so it is in other Animals, we find by their being so seldom afflicted with Mens Distempers, deriv'd from the Causes above-mention-ed: And if the many Diseases of *Horses* seem to ‖ contradict it, I am apt to think it much imputa-ble to the Rack and Manger, the dry and wither'd Stable Com-

---

† Plin. *Nat. Hist. l.* 3. *c.* 12.
‖ Hanc brevitatem Vitæ *(speaking of Horses)* fortasse homini debet,*Verul. Hist.*Vit. & Mort. *See this throughly controverted,* Macrob. Saturn. l. vii. c. v.

mons,

mons, which they muſt eat or
ſtarve, however qualified ; being reſtrained from their Natural
and Spontaneous Choice, which
Nature and Inſtinct directs them
to: To theſe add the Cloſeneſs
of the Air, ſtanding in an almoſt
continu'd Poſture ; beſides the
fulſome Drenches, unſeaſonable
Watrings, and other Practices of
ignorant *Horſe-Quacks* and ſurly
Grooms: The Tyranny and cruel
Uſage of their Maſters in tiring
Journeys, hard, labouring and un-
merciful Treatment, Heats, Colds,
&c. which wear out and deſtroy
ſo many of thoſe uſeful and generous Creatures before the
time : Such as have been better
us'd , and ſome, whom their
more gentle and good-natur'd
Patrons have in recompence of
their long and faithful Service,
diſmiſs'd, and ſent to Paſture for
the reſt of their Lives (as the
Grand-Seignior does his *Meccha-*
Ca-

Camel) have been known to live *forty, fifty*, nay (fays * *Ariftotle*, no fewer than *fixty five* Years. When once Old *Par* came to change his fimple, homely Diet, to that of the *Court* and *Arundel-Houfe*, he quickly funk and dropt away : For, as we have fhew'd, the Stomack eafily concocts plain, and familiar Food ; but finds it an hard and difficult Task, to vanquifh and overcome Meats of || different Subftances : Whence we fo often fee temperate and abftemious Perfons, of a Collegiate Diet, very healthy ; Hufbandmen and laborious People, more robuft, and longer liv'd than others of an uncertain extravagant Diet.

---

* Arift. *Hift. Animal. l.* v. *c.* 14.
|| ἀνόμοια ϛαϛιάζει.

——*Nam*

*———— *Nam variæ res*
Ut noceant Homini, credas, memor
    illius escæ,
Quæ simplex olim tibi sederit ——

For different Meats do hurt ; Remember how
When to one Dish confin'd, thou
    healthier wast than now :

was *Osellus's Memorandum* in the Poet.

Not that Variety (which God has certainly ordain'd to delight and assist our Appetite) is unnecessary , nor any thing more grateful, refreshing and proper for those especially who lead sedentary and studious Lives ; Men of deep Thought, and such as are otherwise disturb'd with Secular Cares and Businesses, which

---

* Hor. *Sat. l.* II. *Sat.* 2. Macr. *Sat. l.* VII.
hin-

hinders the Function of the Stomach and other Organs : whilst those who have their Minds free, use much Exercise, and are more active, create themselves a natural Appetite, which heeds little or no Variety to quicken and content it.

And here might we attest the *Patriarchal* World , nay, and many Persons since ; who living very temperately came not much short of the *Post-Diluvians* themselves , counting from *Abraham* to this Day; and some exceeding them, who liv'd in pure Air, a constant, tho' course and simple Diet; wholsome and uncompounded Drink ; that never tasted *Brandy* or *Exotic Spirits* ; but us'd moderate Exercise, and observ'd good Hours : For such a one a curious Missionary tells us of in *Persia* ; who had attain'd the Age of *four hundred* Years, (a full *Century* beyond the fa-

famous *Johannes de Temporibus*)
and was living *Anno* 1636, and
so may be still for ought we know.
But, to our *Sallet.*

Certain it is, Almighty God
ordaining * *Herbs* and *Fruit* for
the Food of Men, speaks not a
Word concerning *Flesh* for two
thousand Years. And when after, by the *Mosaic* Constitution,
there were Distinctions and Pro-
hibitions about the legal Un-
cleanness of *Animals* ; *Plants,*
of what kind soever, were left
free and indifferent for every
one to choose what best he lik'd.
And what if it was held undecent
and unbecoming the Excellency
of Man's Nature, before Sin en-
tred, and grew enormously wic-
ked, that any Creature should
be put to Death and Pain
for him who had such infinite

---

* Gen. ix

L   store

store of the most delicious and
nourishing Fruit to delight, and
the Tree of Life to sustain him?
Doubtless there was no need of it.
Infants sought the Mother's Nipple as soon as born; and when
grown, and able to feed themselves, run naturally to *Fruit*,
and still will choose to eat it rather than Flesh and certainly
might so persist to do, did not
Custom prevail, even against the
very Dictates of Nature: Nor,
question I, but that what the
Heathen † *Poets* recount of the
Happiness of the *Golden Age*,
sprung from some Tradition
they had received of the *Paradisian* Fare, their innocent and
healthful Lives in that delightful Garden. Let it suffice, that
Adam, and his yet innocent Spouse,
fed on Vegetables and other Hor-

---

† Metam. 1. Fab. iii. *and* xv.

tulan

tulan Productions before the fatal Lapse ; which, by the way, many Learned Men will hardly allow to have fallen out so soon as those imagine who scarcely grant them a single Day ; nay, nor half a one, for their Continuance in the State of Original Perfection ; whilst the sending him into the Garden ; Instructions how he should keep and cultivate it ; Edict, and Prohibition concerning the *Sacramental* Trees; the Imposition of * Names, so apposite to the Nature of such an Infinity of **Living** Creatures (requiring deep Inspection) the Formation of *Eve*, a meet Companion to relieve his Solitude ; the Solemnity of their Marriage ; the Dialogues and Success of the crafty Tempter, whom we cannot reasonably think made but one

---

* Gen. xi. 19.

Af-

Aſſault : And that they ſhould ſo
quickly forget the Injunction of
their Maker and Benefactor; break
their Faith and Faſt, and all o-
ther their Obligations in ſo few
Moments. I ſay, all theſe Par-
ticulars conſider'd ; Can it be
ſuppoſed they were ſo ſoon tranſ-
acted as thoſe do fancy, who
take their Meaſure from the Sum-
mary *Moſes* gives us , who did
not write to gratifie Mens Curio-
ſity, but to tranſmit what was
neceſſary and ſufficient for us to
know.

This then premis'd (as I ſee
no Reaſon why it ſhould not)
and that during all this Space they
liv'd on *Fruits* and *Sallets* ; 'tis
little probable, that after their
Tranſgreſſion , and that they had
forfeited their Dominion over
the Creature (and were ſen-
tenc'd and exil'd to a Life of
Sweat and Labour on a curſed
and ungrateful Soil) the offend
ed

ed God should regale them
with Pampering *Flesh*, or so
much as suffer them to slay the
more innocent Animal : Or,
that if at any time they had
Permission, it was for any thing
save Skins to cloath them, or in
way of Adoration, or *Holocaust*
for Expiation, of which nothing
of the *Flesh* was to be eaten.
Nor did the Brutes themselves
subsist by Prey (tho' pleas'd perhaps with Hunting, without de-
stroying their Fellow Creatures) as
may be presum'd from their long
Seclusion of the most Carnivorous among them in the Ark.

Thus then for two thousand
Years, the Universal Food was
Herbs and *Plants* ; which abun-
dantly recompens'd the Want of
Flesh and other luxurious Meats,
which shortened their Lives so
many hundred Years ; the * μα-
κροβιότια of the Patriarchs, which

---

* *Gen.* ix.

was

was an Emblem of Eternity as it were (after the new Conceſsion) beginning to dwindle to a little Span, a Nothing in Compariſon.

On the other ſide, examine we the preſent Uſages of ſeveral other Heathen Nations ; particularly (beſides the *Ægyptian* Prieſts of old) the *Indian Bramins,* Relicts of the ancient *Gymnoſophiſts* to this Day, obſerving the Inſtitutions of their Founder. *Fleſh,* we know was baniſh'd the *Platonic* Tables, as well as from thoſe of *Pythagoras*; (See †*Porphyry* and their Diſciples) tho' on different Accounts. Among others of the Philoſophers, from *Xenocrates, Polemon,* &c. we hear of many. The like we find in **Clement Alexand.* † *Euſebius* names more. *Zeno, Archinomus, Phraartes, Chi-*

---

† *Porphyr.* de Abſtin. *Proclum, Jambleum,* &c.
**Strom.* vii. † Præp. Ev. paſſim.

ron,

ron, and others, whom *Laertius* reckons up. In ſhort, ſo very many, eſpecially of the Chriſtian Profeſſion, that ſome, even of the ancient * Fathers themſelves, have almoſt thought that the Permiſſion of eating Fleſh to *Noah* and his Sons, was granted them no otherwiſe than *Repudiation* of Wives was to the *Jews*, namely, for *the Hardneſs of their Hearts*, and to ſatisfie a murmuring Generation that a little after loathed *Manna* it ſelf, and *Bread from Heaven*. So difficult a thing it is to ſubdue an unruly Appetite ; which notwithſtanding ‖ *Seneca* thinks not ſo hard a Task ; where ſpeaking of the Philoſopher *Sextius*, and *Socion*'s (abhorring Cruelty and Intemperance) he celebrates the

---

* Tertul. *de Jejun.* cap. iv. Hieron. *adverſ.* Jovin. ‖ Sen. *Epiſt.* 108.

Ad-

Advantages of the *Herby* and
Sallet Diet, as *Physical*, and *Natural* Advancers of Health and other Bleſſings; whilſt Abſtinence
from Fleſh deprives Men of nothing but what *Lions, Vultures,*
Beaſts and Birds of Prey, blood
and gorge themſelves withal.
The whole *Epiſtle* deſerves the
Reading, for the excellent Advice he gives on this and other
Subjects; and how from many
troubleſome and ſlaviſh Impertinencies, grown into Habit and
Cuſtom (old as he was) he had
Emancipated and freed himſelf:
Be this apply'd to our preſent exceſſive Drinkers of Foreign and
Exotic Liquors. And now

I am ſufficiently ſenſible how
far, and to how little purpoſe I
am gone on this *Topic*: The Ply
is long ſince taken, and our
raw *Sallet* deckt in its beſt
Trim, is never like to invite Men
who once have taſted *Fleſh* to
quit

quit and abdicate a Custom
which has now so long obtain'd.
Nor truly do I think Conscience
at all concern'd in the Matter,
upon any Account of Distinction
of *Pure* and *Impure* ; tho' seri-
ously consider'd (as *Sextius* held)
rationi magis congrua, as it regards the cruel Butcheries of so
many harmless Creatures ; some
of which we put to merciless and
needless Torment, to accommodate them for exquisite and un-
common *Epicurism.* There lies
else no positive Prohibition ;
Discrimination of Meats being
* condemn'd as the *Doctrine of
Devils :* Nor do Meats *commend
us to God.* One eats *quid vult* (of
every thing:) another *Olera,* and
of *Sallets* only : But this is not
my Business, further than to

---

* 1 *Cor.* viii. 8.   1 *Tim.* iv. 1. 3. 14.
Rom. ii. 3.

shew

ſhew how poſſible it is by ſo
many Inſtances and Examples, to
live on wholſome Vegetables,
both long and happily : For ſo

* *The* Golden Age, *with this Pro-
viſion bleſt,*
Such a Grand Sallet *made, and
was a Feaſt.*
The Demi-Gods *with Bodies large
and ſound,*
*Commended then the Product of the
Ground.*
*Fraud then, nor Force were known,
nor filthy Luſt,*
*Which Over-heating and Intem-
p'rance nurſt :*
*Be their vile Names in Execration
held,*

---

*Has Epulas habuit teneri gens aurea mundi,
Et cœnæ ingentis tunc caput ipſa ſui.
Semideumque meo creverunt corpora ſucco,
Materiam tanti ſanguinis ille dedit.
Tunc neque fraus nota eſt, neque vis, neque
fœda libido ;
Hæc nimis proles ſæva caloris erat.
Sit ſacrum illorum, ſit deteſtabile nomen,
Qui primi ſervæ regna dedere gulæ.

Who*

*Who with foul Glutt'ny first the
World defil'd :*

Parent of Vice, and all Diseases since,

*With ghastly Death sprung up alone
from thence.*

*Ah, from such reeking, bloody Ta-
bles fly,*

*Which Death for our Destruction
does supply.*

In Health , *if* Sallet Herbs *you
can't endure* ;

Sick, you'll desire them ; *or for*
Food, *or* Cure.

As to the other part of the
Controversie, which concerns us,
αίματοφάγοι, and *Occidental Blood-
Eaters* ; some Grave and Learn'd
Men of late seem to scruple
the present Usage, whilst they

<hr />

Hinc vitiis patefacta via est, morbisq; securis
  Se lethi facies exeruere novæ.   (sas,
Ah, fuge crudeles Animantum sanguine men-
  Quasque tibi obsonat mors inimica dapes.
Poscas tandem æger, si sanus negligis, herbas.
  Esse cibus nequeunt ? at medicamen erunt.
    Colci Plaut. *lib.* I. La&ctuca.

see

see the Prohibition appearing,
and to carry such a Face of *An-*
tiquity, * *Scripture,* † *Councils,*
|| *Canons,* ∴ *Fathers; Imperial*
Constitutions, and *Universal Pra-*
ctice, unless it be among us of these
Tracts of *Europe,* whither, with
other Barbarities, that of eating the
Blood and *Animal*Life of Creatures
first was brought; and by our
Mixtures with the*Goths, Vandals,*
and other Spawn of Pagan *Scy-*
thians; grown a Custom, and since
which I am persuaded more Blood
has been shed between *Christians*
than there ever was before the
Water of the Flood covered this
Corner of the World: Not
that I impute it only to our eating *Blood;* but sometimes wonder how it hapned that so strict,

---

* Gen. ix. † Ancyra xiv. || Can. Apost.
50 ∴ Clem. Pædag. *Lib* ii. *c* i. *Vide* Prudent. *Hymn.* καθημερινῶν : Nos Oloris Coma,
nos siliqua facta legumine multitudo paraveris
innocuis Epulis.

so solemn and famous a *Sanction* not upon a *Ceremonial* Account ; but (as some affirm) a *Moral* and *Perpetual* from *Noah*, to whom the Concession of eating *Flesh* was granted, and that of Blood forbidden (nor to this Day once revok'd) and whilst there also seems to lie fairer Proofs than for most other Controversies agitated among *Christians*, should be so generally forgotten, and give place to so many other impertinent Disputes and Cavels about other superstitious Fopperies, which frequently end in Blood and cutting of Throats.

As to the Reason of this Prohibition, its favouring of Cruelty excepted, (and that by *Galen*, and other experienc'd Physicians, the eating Blood is condemn'd as unwholsome, causing Indigestion and Obstructions) if a positive Command of *Almighty God* were not enough, it seems sufficiently in-

intimated; because *Blood* was the *Vehicle* of the *Life* and *Animal Soul* of the Creature: For what other mysterious Cause, as haply its being always dedicated to *Expiatory Sacrifices*, &c. it is not for us to enquire. 'Tis said, that *Justin Martyr* being asked, why the *Christians* of his time were permitted the eating *Flesh* and not the *Blood*? readily answer'd, That God might distinguish them from Beasts, which eat them both together. 'Tis likewise urg'd, that by the *Apostolical Synod* (when the rest of the *Jewish* Ceremonies and Types were abolish'd) this Prohibition was mention'd as a thing * *necessary*, and rank'd with *Idolatry*, which was not to be local or temporary; but universally injoyn'd to converted Strangers

† Quæst. & Resp. ad Orthod. *Tho. Bartholinus,* de usu Sanguinis.
* xv *Acts,* 20, 29.

and

and *Proselytes,* as well as *Jews :*
Nor could the Scandal of negle-
&ting to observe it, concern them
alone, after so many Ages as it
was and still is in continual
Use; and those who transgress'd,
so severely punish'd, as by an
Imperial Law to be scourg'd to
Blood and Bone : Indeed, so ter-
rible was the Interdiction, that
Idolatry excepted (which was also Moral and perpetual) nothing
in Scripture seems to be
more express. In the mean
time, to relieve all other
Scruples, it does not, they
say, extend to that ἀκρίβεια of
those few diluted Drops of *Ex-
travasated Blood*, which might
happen to tinge the Juice and
Gravy of the Flesh (which were
indeed *to strain at a Gnat*) but to
those who devour the *Venal* and
Arterial Blood separately, and in
Quantity, as a choice Ingredient
of their luxurious Preparations
and *Apician* Tables. But

But this, and all the rest will, I
fear, seem but *Oleribus verba fa-
cere*, and (as the Proverb goes)
be Labour-in-vain to think of
preaching down *Hogs-Puddings*,
and usurp the Chair of *Rabby-
Busy:* And therefore what is
advanc'd in Countenance of the
Antediluvian Diet, we leave to
be ventilated by the Learned,
and such as *Curcellæus*, who has
borrow'd of all the Ancient
Fathers, from *Tertullian, Hierom,
S. Chrysostom,* &c. to the later
Doctors and Divines, *Lyra, To-
ſtatus, Dionyſius Carthuſianus, Pe-
rerius,* amongst the *Pontificians* ;
of *Peter Martyr, Zanchy, Areti-
us, Jac. Capellus, Hiddiger, Coc-
ceius, Bochartus,* &c. amongst the
Proteſtants ; and *inſtar omnium,*
by *Salmaſius, Grotius , Voſſius ,
Blundel :* In a Word, by the
Learn'd of both Persuasions ,
favourable enough to these Opi-
nions, *Cajetan* and *Calvin* only excepted,

cepted, who hold, that as to *Abstinence* from *Flesh*, there was no
positive Command or Imposition
concerning it; but that the Use
of *Herbs* and *Fruit* was recom-
mended rather for Temperance
sake, and the Prolongation of
Life: Upon which score I am
inclin'd to believe that the ancient Θεραπεύται, and other devout
and contemplative Sects, distinguish'd themselves; whose Course
of Life we have at large describ'd
in * *Philo* (who liv'd and taught
much in Gardens) with others of
the Abstemious *Christians*; a-
mong whom, *Clemens* brings in
St. *Mark* the *Evangelist* himself,
James our Lord's Brother, St.
John, &c. and with several of
the devout Sex, the famous
Diaconesse Olympias, mention'd
by *Palladius* (not to name the

---

* *Philo* de Vit. Contemp. *Joseph.* Antiq. *Lib.*
13. *Cap.* 9.

M   rest)

rest) who abstaining from Flesh, betook themselves to *Herbs* and *Sallets* upon the Account of Temperance, and the Vertues accompanying it ; and concerning which the incomparable *Grotius* declares ingenuously his Opinion to be far from censuring, not only those who forbear the eating *Flesh* and Blood, *Experimenti Causâ*, and for Discipline sake ; but such as forbear *ex Opinione,* and (because it has been the ancient Custom) provided they blam'd none who freely us'd their Liberty ; and I think he's in the right.

But leaving this Controversie (*nè nimium extra oleas*) it has often been objected, that *Fruit*, and *Plants*, and all other things, may since the Beginning, and as the World grows older, have universally become *Effæte*, impair'd and divested of those Nutritious and transcendent Vertues they were

at

at firſt endow'd withal : But as this is begging the Queſtion, and to which we have already ſpoken ; ſo all are not agreed that there is any, the leaſt * *Decay in Nature,* where equal Induſtry and Skill's apply'd. 'Tis true indeed, that the *Ordo Foliatorum, Feuillantines* (a late Order of *Aſcetic Nuns*) amongſt other Mortifications, made Trial upon the *Leaves* of *Plants* alone, to which they would needs confine themſelves ; but were not able to go through that thin and meagre Diet : But then it would be enquir'd whether they had not firſt, and from their very Childhood, been fed and brought up with *Fleſh*, and better Suſtenance till they enter'd the *Cloyſter* ; and what the Vegetables and the Preparation of

---

* *Hackwell.* Apolog.

　　　　　　　　them

them were allow'd by their Institution? Wherefore this is nothing to our Modern Use of *Sallets*, or its Disparagement. In the mean time, that we still think it not only possible, but likely, and with no great Art or Charge (taking *Roots* and *Fruit* into the Basket) substantially to maintain Mens Lives in Health and Vigour: For to *this*, and less than this, we have the Suffrage of the great || *Hippocrates* himself; who thinks, *ab initio etiam hominum* (as well as other Animals) *tali victu usum esse*, and needed no other Food. Nor is it an inconsiderable Speculation, That since *all Flesh is Grass* (not in a *Figurative*, but *Natural* and *Real* Sense) *Man* himself, who lives on *Flesh*, and I think upon no Earthly Animal whatsoever,

---

|| *Hippoc. de vetere Medicina, Cap.* 6, 7.

but

but such as feed on Grass, is nourish'd with them still; and so becoming an *Incarnate Herb*, and
Innocent *Canibal*, may truly be
said to devour himself.

We have said nothing of the
Lotophagi, and such as (like St.
John the *Baptist*, and other religi-
ous *Ascetics*) were Feeders on the
Summities and Tops of Plants:
But as divers of those, and o-
thers we have mention'd, were
much in times of Streights, Per-
secutions, and other Circumstances, which did not in the least
make it a Pretence, exempting
them from Labour, and other
Humane Offices, by ensnaringOb-
ligations and *Vows* (never to be
useful to the Publick, in whatever
Exigency) so I cannot but take
Notice of what a Learned ‖ *Critic*
speaking of Mens neglecting
plain and Essential Duties, under
Colour of exercising themselves

‖ L. C. *Annot. in* Coloss. *c.* 2.

in

in a more sublime Course of Piety, and being Righteous above what is commanded (as those who seclude themselves in Monasteries) that they manifestly discover excessive Pride, Hatred of their Neighbour, Impatience of Injuries ; to which *add*, *Melancholy Plots and Machinations* ; and that he must be either stupid, or infected with the same Vice himself, who admires this ἐθελοπερισσοθρήσκεια , or thinks they were for that Cause the more pleasing to God. This being so, what may we then think of such Armies of *Hermits* , *Monks* and *Fryars*, who pretending to justifie a mistaken Zeal and meritorious Abstinence ; not only by a peculiar Diet and Distinction of Meats (which God without Distinction has made the moderate Use of common and * indifferent amongst *Christians*) but by other sordid Usages, and unnecessary

* 2 *Tim.* iv. 3.

Hard-

Hardſhips, wilfully prejudice
their Health and Conſtitution?
and through a ſingular manner
of living, dark and *Saturnine*;
whilſt they would ſeem to abdicate and forſake the World (in
Imitation, as they pretend, of the
Ancient *Eremites*) take care to
ſettle, and build their warm and
ſtately Neſts in the moſt Populous
Cities, and Places of Reſort;
ambitious doubtleſs of the Peo-
ples Veneration and Opinion of
an extraordinary Sanctity; and
therefore flying the *Deſarts*, where
there is indeed no uſe of them;
and flocking to the *Towns* and
Cities where there is leſs, indeed
none at all; and therefore no
Marvel that the Emperour *Valen-
tinian* baniſhed them the Cities,
and *Conſtantine Copronymus* finding them ſeditious, oblig'd them
to marry, to leave their Cells,
and live as did others. For of
theſe, ſome there are who ſeldom

ſpeak

speak, and therefore edifie none;
sleep little, and lie hard, are
clad nastily, and eat meanly (and
oftentimes that which is unwholsom) and therefore benefit none:
Not because they might not, both
for their own, and the Good of
others, and the Publick; but because they will not; Custom, and
a prodigious † Sloth accompanying it; which renders it so far
from *Penance*, and the Mortifi-
cation pretended, that they know
not how to live, or spend their
Time otherwise. This, as I have
often consider'd, so was I glad
to find it justly perstring'd, and
taken notice of by a * Learned
Person, amongst others of his useful Remarks abroad.

'These, says he, willingly re-
' nouncing the innocent Com-
' forts of Life, plainly shew it

† *This, with their prodigious Ignorance.* See
Mab. des Etudes Monast. *Part.* 2. *c.* 17.
* *Dr.* Lister's *Journey to* Paris. See *L' Apocalyps de*
Meliton, *ou Revelation des Mysteres Cenobitiques.*

' to

' to proceed more from a chagrin
' and morose Humour, than from
' any true and serious Principle of
' sound Religion ; which teaches
' Men to be useful in their Gene-
' rations, sociable and commu-
' nicative, unaffected, and by no
' means singular and fantastic in
' Garb and Habit, as are these
' (forsooth) Fathers (as they af-
' fect to be call'd) spending their
Days in idle and fruitless Forms,
and tedious Repetitions ; and
thereby thinking to merit the
Reward of those Ancient, and
truly pious *Solitaries*, who, God
knows, were driven from their
Countries and Repose, by the
Incursions of barbarous Nations
(whilst these have no such Cause)
and compell'd to Austerities,
not of their own chusing and
making, but the publick Calami-
ty ; and to *labour* with their
Hands for their own, and others
necessary Support, as well as
with

with their *Prayers* and holy
Lives, Examples to all the
World: And some of these indeed (besides the *Solitaries* of
the *Thebaid*, who wrought for
abundance of poor Christians,
sick, and in Captivity). I might
bring in, as such who deserv'd to
have their Names preserv'd; not
for their rigorous Fare, and un-
couth Disguises; but for teach-
ing that the Grace of Temperance and other Vertues, consist-
ed in a cheerful, innocent, and
profitable Conversation.

And now to recapitulate
what other Prerogatives the
Hortulan Provision has been celebrated for, besides its Anti-
quity, Health and *Longævity* of
the *Antediluvians*; that Temperance, Frugality, Leisure,
Ease, and innumerable other
Vertues and Advantages, which
accompany it, are no less attributable to it. Let us hear
our

our excellent *Botanist* * Mr.
Ray.

'The Use of Plants (says he)
'is all our Life long of that uni-
'versal Importance and Concern;
'that we can neither live nor sub-
'sist in any Plenty with Decency,
'orConveniency or be said to live
'indeed at all without them:what-
'soeverFood is necessary to sustain
'us, whatsoever contributes to
'delight and refresh us, are sup-
'ply'd and brought forth out of
'that plentiful and abundantstore:
'and ah,how much more innocent,
'sweet and healthful, is a Table
'cover'd with these, than with
'all the reeking Flesh of butcher'd

---

* Plantarum usus latissimè patet, & in om-
ni vitæ parte occurrit , sine illis lautè, sine
illis commodè non vivitur, ac nec vivitur
omninò. Quæcunque ad victu necessaria
sunt, quæcunque ad delicias faciunt, è locu-
pletissimo suo penu abundè subministrant:
Quantò ex eis mensa innocentior, mundior,
salubrior, quam ex animalium cæde & Lani-

'and

'and slaughter'd Animals ! Cer-
'tainly Man by Nature was ne-
'ver made to be a *Carnivorous*
'Creature ; nor is he arm'd at
'all for Prey and Rapin, with
'gag'd and pointed Teeth and
'crooked Claws , sharpned to
'rend and tear : But with gentle
'Hands to gather Fruit and Ve-
'getables, and with Teeth to chew
'and eat them : Nor do we so
'much as read the Use of *Flesh* for
'Food, was at all permitted him,
'till after the Universal De-
'luge, *&c.*

To this might we add that
transporting Consideration, becoming both our Veneration and

---

ena ! Homo certè naturâ animal carnivorum
non est;nullis ad prædam & rapinam armis in-
structum;non dentibus exertis & serratis, non
unguibus aduncis : Manus ad fructos colli-
gendos, dentes ad mandendos comparati ;
nec legimus se ante diluvium carnes ad esum
concessas, &c. *Raii Hist. Plant. Lib. 1. cap. 24.*

Ad-

Admiration of the infinitely
wise and glorious Author of
Nature, who has given to *Plants*
such astonishing Properties; such
fiery Heat in some to warm and
cherish, such Coolness in others
to temper and refresh, such pinguid Juice to nourish and feed
the Body, such quickening *Acids*
to compel the Appetite, and
grateful Vehicles to court the
Obedience of the Palate, such
Vigour to renew and support our
natural Strength, such ravishing
Flavour and Perfumes to recre-
ate and delight us : In short, such
spirituous and active Force to a-
nimate and revive every Faculty and Part, to all the kinds of
Human, and, I had almost said
Heavenly Capacity too. What
shall we add more ? Our Gardens present us with them all ;
and whilst the *Shambles* are cover'd with Gore and Stench, our
Sallets scape the Insults of the
Sum-

Summer *Fly*, purifies and warms the Blood againſt Winter Rage: Nor wants there Variety in more abundance, than any of the former Ages could ſhew.

Survey we their *Bills of Fare*, and Numbers of Courſes ſerv'd up by *Athenæus*, dreſt with all the Garniſh of *Nicander* and o-ther *Grecian* Wits : What has the *Roman Grand Sallet* wo rth the naming ? *Parat Convivium*, The Gueſts are nam'd indeed, and we are told,

—— * *Varias, quas habet hortus*
  opes ?
How richly the Garden's ſtor'd !

In quibus eſt Luctuca ſedens , &
  tonſile porrum,
Nec deeſt ructatrix Mentha, nec
  herba ſalax, &c.
  A Goodly Sallet !

---

* Mart. *lib.* x. *Epig.* 44.

Lettuce, Leeks, Mint, Rocket, Colewort-Tops, with *Oyl* and *Eggs,* and such an *Hotch-Pot* following (as the Cook in *Plautus* would deservedly laugh at) But how infinitely out-done in this Age of ours, by the Variety of so many rare *Edules* unknown to the Ancients, that there's no room for the Comparison. And, for Magnificence, let the *Sallet* drest by the Lady for an Entertainment made by *Jacobus Catsius* (describ'd by the Poet * *Barlæus*)shew;not at all yet out-doing what we every Day almost find at our *Lord Mayor's Table,* and other great Persons, Lovers of the Gardens ; that sort of elegant Cookery being capable of such wonderful Variety , tho' not altogether wanting of old, if that be true which is related to

---

* Barl. *Eleg. lib.* 3.

us

us of ‖ *Nicomedes* a certain King
of *Bithynia*, whose Cook made
him a *Pilchard* (a Fish he exceedingly long'd for) of a well dis-
sembl'd *Turnip*, carv'd in its
Shape, and drest with *Oyl*, *Salt*,
and *Pepper*, that so deceiv'd,
and yet pleased the Prince,
that he commended it for the best
Fish he had ever eaten. Nor
does all this exceed what every
industrious *Gardiner* may inno-
cently enjoy, as well as the
greatest Potentate on Earth.

Vitellius *his Table, to which eve-
ry Day*
All *Courtiers did a constant Tribute
pay,*
Could *nothing more delicious afford
Than Nature's Liberality.*
Help'd *with a little Art and Industry,
Allows the meanest Gard'ners Board,*

‖ Athen. Deip. *l.* 1.

The wanton Taste no Fish or Fowl
   can chuse,
For which the Grape or Melon she
   would lose.
Tho' all th' Inhabitants of Sea and
   Air.
Be listed in the Glutton's Bill of
   Fare ;
Yet still the Sallet, *and the* Fruit
   we see
Plac'd the third Story high in all
   her Luxury.

So the Sweet † *Poet,* whom I can
never part with for his Love to
this delicious Toil, and the Honour he has done me.

   Verily, the infinite Plenty and
Abundance, with which the be-
nign and bountiful Author of
Nature has stor'd the whole Ter-
restrial World, more with *Plants*
and *Vegetables* than with any o-

---

† Cowley, *Garden. Stanz. 6.*

    N   ther

ther Provision whatsoever; and
the Variety not only equal, but
by far exceeding the Pleasure and
Delight of Taste (above all the
Art of the *Kitchen*, than ever
* *Apicius* knew) seems loudly to
call, and kindly invite all her
living Inhabitants (none excepted) who are of gentle Nature,
and most useful, to the same
Hospitable and Common-Board ,
which first she furnish'd with
Plants and *Fruit*, as to their natural and genuine Pasture ; nay,
and of the most wild, and sa-
vage too *ab origine :* As in *Paradise* , where, as the *Evangeli-
cal* † Prophet adumbrating the

---

* *Hence in* Macrobius Sat. lib. vii. c. 5
we find Eupolis *the Comedian in his* Æges, *bring-
ing in Goats boasting the Variety of their Food,*
Βοσκόμεθ ὕλης ἀπὸ παντοδαπῆς, ἐλάτης, &c.
After which follows a Banquet *of innumerable
sorts*

† Esa. lxv. 25.

fu-

future Glory of the *Catholick Church*, (of which that happy *Garden* was the *Antitype*) the *Wolf and the Lamb, the angry and furious Lion, should eat Grass and Herbs together with the Ox.* But after all, *latet anguis in herba*, there's a *Snake* in the Grass; Luxury, and Excess in our most innocent Fruitions. There was a time indeed when the Garden furnish'd Entertainments for the most Renown'd Heroes, virtuous and excellent Persons; till the Blood-thirsty and Ambitious, over-running the Nations, and by Murders and Rapine rifl'd the World, to transplant its Luxury to its new Mistriss, *Rome*. Those whom heretofore * two Acres

---

* Bina tunc jugera populo Romano satis erat, nullíque majorem modum attribuit, quo servos paulo ante principis Neronis, contemptis hujus spatii Viridariis, piscinas juvat habere majores, gratúmque, si non aliquem & culinas. *Plin. Hist. Nat. lib.* xviii. *c.* 2.

of

of Land would have satisfied,
and plentifully maintain'd; had
afterwards their very Kitchens
almost as large as their first Ter-
ritories: Nor was that enough:
Entire * *Forests* and *Parks*, *War-
rens* and *Fish-Ponds*, and ample
Lakes to furnish their Tables,
so as Men could not live by one
another without Oppression:
Nay, and to shew how the best,
and most innocent things may be
perverted; they chang'd those
frugal and *inemptas Dapes* of their
Ancestors, to that Height and
Profusion; that we read of * *E-
dicts* and *Sumptuary Laws*, enact-
ed to restrain even the Pride and
Excess of *Sallets*. But so it was
not when the *Pease-Field* spread

---

* Interea gustus elementa per omnia quæ-
runt. *Juv. Sat.* 4.

† Cicero. *Epist.* Lib. 7: *Ep.* 26. *Complaining
of a costly Sallet, that had almost cost him his
Life.*

a

a Table for the Conquerors of
the World, and their Grounds
were cultivated *Vomere laureato,*
& triumphali aratore : The greatest Princes took the *Spade* and
the *Plough-Staff* in the same Hand
they held the Sceptre ; and the
Noblest † Families thought it no
Dishonour, to derive their Names
from *Plants* and *Sallet-Herbs* :
They arriv'd, I say to that
Pitch of ingrossing all that
was but green, and could be
vary'd by the Cook (*Heu quam*
prodiga ventris !) that, as *Pliny*
tells us (*non sine pudore,* not
without blushing) a poor Man
could hardly find a *Thistle* to
dress for his Supper ; or what

---

† Valeriana, *That of* Lectucini, Achil-
leia, Lysimachia. Fabius , Cicero, Len-
tulus, Piso, &c. à Fabis, Cicere, Lente, Pisis
bene serendis dicti, *Plin.*

his

his hungry * *Ass* would not touch, for fear of pricking his Lips.

Verily the Luxury of the East ruin'd the greatest Monarchies ; first, the *Persian*, then the *Grecian*, and afterwards *Rome* her self : By what Steps, see elegantly describ'd in Old || *Gratius* the *Faliscian*, deploring his own Age compar'd with the former :

O quantum, & quoties decoris fru-
strata paterni !
At qualis nostris, quàm simplex men-
sa Camillis !
Qui tibi cultus erat post tot, serrane,
triumphos ?
Ergo illi ex habitu, virtutisq; indole
priscæ,
Imposuere orbi Romam caput :——

---

* Mirum esset non licere pecori Carduis vesci, non licet plebei, &c. *And in another Place,* Quoniam portenta quoque terrarum in ganeam vertimus, etiam quæ refugeant quadrupedes consciæ, *Plin.* Hist. Nat. l. xix. c. 8.
|| Gra. Falisc. *Cyneget.* Was. *See concerning this Excess* Macr. *Sat. l.* 2. *c.* 9. & sequ.

Neigh-

Neighb'ring   Excesses   being
    made thine own,
How art thou fall'n from thine
    old Renown!
But our *Camilli* did but plainly
    fare ,
No Port did oft triumphant *Ser-*
    ran bear :
Therefore such Hardship, and
    their Heart so great
Gave *Rome* to be the World's
    Imperial Seat.

But as these were the Sensual
and Voluptuous, who abus'd
their Plenty, spent their Fortunes
and shortned their Lives by their
Debauches; so never did they taste
the Delicaces, and true Satisfaction
of a sober Repast, and the
infinite Conveniences of what
well-stor'd *Garden* affords ;
so elegantly describ'd by the
        N 4   * *Natu-*

* *Naturalift,* as cofting neither
Fuel nor Fire to boil, Pains or
time to gather and prepare, *Res
expedita & parata femper:* All
was fo near at hand, readily dreft,
and of fo eafie Digeftion ; as neither to offend the Brain, or dull
the Senfes ; and in the greateft
Dearth of Corn, a little Bread fuf-
fic'd. In all Events,

|| *Panis ematur, Olus, Vini Sextari-
us adde*

*Queis humana fibi doleat natura
negatis.*

Bread, Wine, and wholfome Sallets you may buy,

What Nature adds befides is Luxury.

---

* Horti maximè placebant, quia non ege-
rent igni, parcerénrque ligno, expedita res,
& parata femper, unde *Acetaria* appellantur,
facilia concoqui, nec oneratura fenium cibo,
& quæ minimè accenderent defiderium panis.
Plin. Hift. Nat. Lib. xix *c.* 4. *And cf this
exceeding Frugality of the* Romans, *till after the*
Mithridatic *War, fee* Athenæus Deip. *Lib.* 6.
cap. 21.

|| Horat. *Serm. Sat.* 1.

They

They could then make an honeſt Meal, and dine upon a *Sallet*, without ſo much as a Grain of *Exotic Spice* ; And the *Potagere* was in ſuch Reputation, that ſhe who neglected her *Kitchen-Garden* (for that was ſtill the Good-Woman's Province) was never reputed a tolerable Huſwife : *Si vespertinus subitò te oppreſſerit hospes*, ſhe was never ſurpriz'd, had all (as we ſaid) at hand, and could in a Trice ſet forth an handſome *Sallet* : And if this was Happineſs, *Convictus facilis ſine arte menſa* (as the *Poet* reckons) it was here in Perfection. In a Word, ſo univerſal was the *Sallet*, that the * Un-bloody Shambles (as *Pliny* calls them) yielded the † *Roman* State a more conſiderable Cuſtom (when there

---

* Nequam eſſe in domo matrem familias (etenim hæc cura Fœminæ dicebatur) ubi indiligens eſſet hortus.

† Alterum ſuccidium. *Cic.* in *Catone.*
Tiberias *had a Tribute of* Skirts *paid him.*

WAS

was little more than honest *Cab-bage* and *Worts*) than almost any thing besides brought to Market.

They spent not then so much precious time as afterwards they did, gorging themselves with *Flesh* and *Fish*, so as hardly able to rise, without reeking and reeling from Table.

*——— *Vides ut pallidus omnis*

Cœna desurgat dubia? quin corpus onustum

Hesternis vitiis, animum quoque prægravat unà,

Atque affigit humo divinæ particulam auræ.

See but how pale they look, how wretchedly,

With Yesterday's Surcharge disturb'd they be!

Nor Body only suff'ring, but the Mind,

That nobler Part, dull'd and depress'd we find.

*Hor. Sat. l. 2. Vix præ vino sustinet palpebras, eunti in consilium, &c. See the Oration of C. Titius de Leg. Fan. Mac. Sat. l. 2. c. 12.

Drow-

Drowſie and unapt for Buſineſs, and other nobler Parts of Life.

Time was before Men in thoſe golden Days : Their Spirits were brisk and lively.

—— *Ubi dicto citius curata ſopori Membra dedit, Vegetus præſcripta ad munera ſurgit.*

With ſhorter, but much ſweeter Sleep content,
Vigorous and freſh, about their Buſineſs went.

And Men had their Wits about them; their Appetites were natural, their Sleep *molli ſub arbore,* ſound, ſweet and kindly : That excellent Emperour *Tacitus* being us'd to ſay of *Lettuce,* that he did *ſomnum ſe mercari* when he eat of them, and call'd it a ſumptuous Feaſt, with a *Sallet* and a ſingle *Pullet,* which was uſually all the Fleſh-Meat that ſober
Prince

Prince eat of; whilst *Maximinus* (a profess'd Enemy to *Sallet*) is reported to have scarce been satisfied, with sixty Pounds of *Flesh*, and Drink proportionable.

There was then also far less expensive Grandure, but far more true State; when *Consuls*, great Statesmen (and such as atchiev'd the most renown'd Actions) sup'd in their *Gardens*; not under costly, gilded, and inlaid Roofs, but the spreading *Platan*; and drank of the Chrystal Brook, and by Temperance, and healthy Frugality, maintain'd the Glory of *Sallets*, *Ah, quanto innocentiore victu!* with what Content and Satisfaction! Nor, as we said, wanted there Variety; for so in the most blissful Place, and innocent State of Nature, See how the first *Empress* of the World *Regal's* her *Celestial* Guest:

*With

*With sav'ry Fruit of Taste to please
True Appetite,——and brings
Whatever Earth's all-bearing Mo-
ther yields
—— Fruit of all kinds, in Coat
Rough, or smooth-Rind, or beard-
ed Husk, or Shell.
Heaps with unsparing Hand : For
Drink the Grape
She crushes, inoffensive Moust, and
Meaches
From many a Berry, and from sweet
Kernel prest,
She temper'd dulcid Creams.——

Then for the Board.

— —— Rais'd of a grassy Turf
The Table was, and Mossy Seats had
round ;
And on the ample Square from Side
to Side,
All Autumn pil'd : Ah Innocence ,
Deserving Paradise !

---

* Milton's Paradise, l. v. ver. 228.

Thus

Thus, the *Hortulan* Provision of the † *Golden Age* fitted all *Places, Times* and *Persons* ; and when Man is restor'd to that State again, it will be as it was in the Beginning.

But now after all (and for Close of all) Let none yet imagine, that whilst we justifie our present Subject through all the *Topics* of *Panegyric*, we would in Favour of the *Sallet*, drest with all its Pomp and Advantage turn Mankind to *Grass* again ; which were ungratefully to neglect the Bounty of Heaven, as well as his Health and Comfort : But by these Noble Instances and Examples, to reproach the *Luxury* of the present Age ; and by shewing the infi-

---

† At victus illa ætas cui fecimus aurea
  nomen
Fructibus arboreis, & quas humus educat
  herbis
Fortunata fuit.————*Met.* xv.

nite

nite Blessing and Effects of Temperance, and the Vertues accompanying it; with how little Nature, and a * Civil Appetite may be happy, contented with moderate things, and within a little Compass, reserving the rest, to the nobler Parts of Life. And thus of old,

Hoc erat in votis, modus agri non
ita magnus, &c.

He that was possess'd of a little Spot of Ground, and well-cultivated *Garden*, with other moderate Circumstances, had ‖*Hæredium*. All that a modest Man could well desire. Then,

---

* Bene moratus venter.
‖ TAB. II.

* *Happy the Man, who from Am-*
    bition freed,
A little Garden, little Field does
    feed.
The Field gives frugal Nature
    what's requir'd;
The Garden what's luxuriously de-
    sir'd:
The specious Evils of an anxious
    Life,
He leaves to Fools to be their end-
    less Strife.

O Fortunatos nimium bona si sua
    norint
Horticulos !

---

* Fœlix, quem miserâ procul ambitione re-
motum,
    Parvus ager placidè, parvus & hortus, alit.
Præbet ager quicquid frugi natura requirit,
    Hortus habet quicquid luxuriosa petit,
Cætera sollicitæ speciosa incommoda vitæ
    Permittit stultis quærere, habere malis.
                            Cowley, Pl. lib. iv.

F I N I S.

APPENDIX.

THO' it was far from our
first Intention to charge
this small Volume and Discourse concerning Crude Sallets,
with any of the following Receits: Yet having since received
them from an Experienc'd House-
wife; and that they may possibly
be useful to correct, preserve and
improve our Acetaria, we have
allow'd them Place as an Appendant Variety upon Occasion: Nor
account we it the least Dishonour
to our former Treatise, that we
kindly entertain'd them; since
(besides divers Learned Physicians, and such as have ex profes-
so written de Re Cibaria) we
have the Examples of many other

O   * No-

Appendix.

Plin. Athenæus, Macrobius, Bacon, Boyle, Digby, &c.

* Noble *and* Illustrious *Persons, both among the* Ancient *and* Modern.

Artichoak. *Clear it of the Leaves and cut the* Bottoms *in pretty thin Slices or Quarters; then fry them in fresh Butter with some Parsley, till it is crisp, and the Slices tender; and so dish them with other fresh melted Butter.*

How a Poiverade *is made, and the Bottoms preserv'd all the Winter,* See Acetaria. *p.* 8, 9.

Ashen-keys. *See* Pickle.
Asparagus. *See* Pickle.

Beets.
Broom. } *See* Pickle.
Buds.
Capers. }

Carrot. *See* Pudding.
Champignon. *See* Mushroom

Ches-

2. **Chessnut.** *Roasted under the Embers, or dry fryed, till they shell, and quit their Husks, may be slit; the Juice of Orange squeezed on a Lump of hard Sugar dissolv'd; to which add some Claret Wine.*

Collyflower.
Cucumber.
Elder-flowers. } *See* Pickle.
Flowers.
Gilly-flowers.

Herbs. *See* Pudding *and* Tart.
Limon. *See* Pickle.

3. **Mushroom.** *Chuse the small, firm and white Buttons, growing upon sweet Pasture Grounds, neither under, or about any Trees: strip off the upper Skin, and pare away all the black spungy Bottom part; then slice them in quarters, and cast them in Water a while to cleanse: Then Boil them in*

O 2　　　*fresh*

Appendix.

fresh Water, and a little sweet Butter; (some boil them a quarter of an hour first) and then taking them out, dry them in a Cloth, pressing out the Water, and whilst hot, add the Butter; and then boiling a full Hour (to exhaust the Malignity) shift them in another clean Water, with Butter, as before till they become sufficiently tender. Then being taken out, pour upon them as much strong Mutton (or other) Broth as will cover them, with six Spoonfuls of White-Wine, twelve Cloves, as many Pepper-Corns, four small young Onions, half an Handful of Persly bound up with two or three Spriggs of Thyme, an Anchovy, Oysters raw, or pickl'd; a little Salt, sweet Butter; and so let them stew. See Acetar. p. 39.

Ano-

Appendix.

Another.

Prepar'd, and cleans'd as above, and cast into Fountain-Water, to preserve them from growing black; Boil them in fresh Water and Salt; and whilst on the Fire, cast in the Mushrooms, letting them boil till they become tender: Then stew them leisurely between two Dishes (the Water being drained from them) in a third Part of White-Wine and Butter, a small Bundle of sweet Herbs at discretion. To these add Broth as before, with Cloves, Mace, Nutmeg, Anchovies (one is sufficient) Oysters, &c. a small Onion, with the green Stem chopt small; and lastly, some Mutton-Gravy, rubbing the Dish gently with a Clove of Garlick, or some Rocombo Seeds in its stead. Some beat the Yolk of a fresh Egg with Vinegar, and Butter, and a little Pepper.

O 3 In

Appendix.

In France *some* (*more compendiously being peel'd and prepared*) cast them into a Pipkin, where, with the Sweet Herbs, Spice, and an Onion they stew them in their own Juice, without any other Water or Liquor at all; and then taking out the Herbs and Onion, thicken it with a little Butter, and so eat them.

In Poiverade.

The large Mushrooms well cleansed, &c. being cut into quarters and strewed with Pepper. and Salt, are broil'd on the Grid-iron, and eaten with fresh Butter.

In Powder.

Being fresh gathered, cleans'd, &c. and cut in Pieces, stew them in Water and Salt; and being taken forth, dry them with a Cloth: Then putting them into an Earth-Glazed Pot, set them into the Oven after the Bread is drawn: Repeat this till they are perfectly dry; and reserve them in Papers

to

Appendix.

to crumble into what Sawce you please. For the rest, see Pickle.

4. Muſtard. *Procure the beſt and weightieſt Seed: caſt it into Water two or three times, till no more of the Husk ariſe: Then taking out the ſound (which will ſink to the Bottom) rub it very dry in warm courſe Cloths, ſhewing it alſo a little to the Fire in a Diſh or Pan. Then ſtamp it as ſmall as to paſs through a fine Tiffany Sieve: Then ſlice ſome Horſe-Raddiſh, and lay it to ſoak in ſtrong Vinegar, with a ſmall Lump of hard Sugar (which ſome leave out) to temper the Flower with, being drained from the Radiſh, and ſo pot it all in a Glaz'd* Mug *, with an Onion, and keep it well ſtop'd with a Cork upon a Bladder, which is the more cleanly: But this* Receit *is improv'd, if inſtead of Vinegar, Water only, or the Broth of powder'd Beef be made uſe of. And to ſome of*

O 4   *this*

this Mustard *adding Verjuice, Sugar, Claret-Wine, and Juice of Limon, you have an excellent Sauce to any sort of Flesh or Fish.*

Note, that a Pint of good Seed is enough to make at one time, and to keep fresh a competent while. What part of it does not pass the Sarse, may be beaten again; and you may reserve the Flower in a well closed Glass, and make fresh Mustard when you please. See Acetaria, *p.* 59. 103.

Nasturtium. *Vide* Pickle.

Orange. *See* Limon *in Pickle.*

5. Parsnip. *Take the large Roots, boil them, and strip the Skin: Then slit them long-ways into pretty thin Slices; Flower and fry them in fresh Butter till they look brown. The Sauce is other sweet Butter melted. Some strow Sugar and Cinamon upon them. Thus you may accommodate other Roots.* There

Appendix.

There is made a Mash or Po-mate of this Root, being boiled very tender with a little fresh Cream ; and being heated again, put to it some Butter, a little Su-gar and Juice of Limon ; dish it upon Sippets ; sometimes a few Corinths *are added.*

Peny-royal. *See* Pudding.

Pickles.

Pickl'd
6. Artichoaks.   *See* Acetaria, p. 9.

7. Ashen-keys *Gather them young, and boil them in three or four Waters to extract the Bitterness ; and when they feel tender , pre-pare a Syrup of sharp White-Wine Vinegar, Sugar, and a little Wa-ter. Then boil them on a very quick Fire, and they will become of a green Colour, fit to be pot-ted so soon as cold.*

8.

Appendix.

8. Asparagus. *Break off the hard Ends and put them in White-Wine Vinegar and Salt, well covered with it; and so let them remain for six Weeks: Then taking them out, boil the Liquour or Pickle, and scum it carefully. If need be, renew the Vinegar and Salt; and when 'tis cold, pot them up again. Thus may one keep them the whole Year.*

9. Beans. *Take such as are fresh young, and approaching their full Growth. Put them into a strong Brine of White-Wine Vinegar and Salt able to bear an Egg. Cover them very close, and so will they be preserved twelve Months: But a Month before you use them, take out what Quantity you think sufficient for your spending a quarter of a Year (for so long the second Pickle will keep them sound) and boil them in a Skillet of fresh Wa-*

Water, till they begin to look *green*, as they soon will do. Then placing them one by one, (to drain upon a clean course *Napkin*) range them *Row* by *Row* in a *Jarr*, and cover them with *Vinegar*, and what *Spice* you please; some *Weight* being laid upon them to keep them under the *Pickle*. Thus you may preserve *French-Beans*, *Harico's*, &c. the whole *Year* about.

10. Broom-Buds and Pods. Make a strong *Pickle*, as above; stir it very well, till the *Salt* be quite dissolved, clearing off the *Dregs* and *Scum*. The next *Day* pour it from the *Bottom*; and having rubbed the *Buds* dry pot them up in a *Pickle-Glass*, which should be frequently shaken, till they sink under it, and keep it well stopt and covered.

Thus may you pickle any other *Buds*. Or as follows:

11.

Appendix.

11. *Of Elder. Take the largest Buds, and boil them in a Skillet with Salt and Water, sufficient only to scald them ; and so (being taken off the Fire) let them remain covered till Green ; and then pot them with Vinegar and Salt, which has had one Boil up to cleanse it.*

12. *Collyflowers. Boil them till they fall in Pieces : Then with some of the Stalk, and worst of the Flower, boil it in a part of the Liquor till pretty strong : Then being taken off, strain it ; and when settled, clear it from the Bottom. Then with Dill, Gross Pepper, a pretty Quantity of Salt, when cold, add as much Vinegar as will make it sharp, and pour all upon the Collyflower ; and so as to keep them from touching one another ; which is prevented by putting Paper close to them.*

Cornelians are pickled like Olives.

13.

Appendix.

13. Cowſlips. *Pickt very clean;
to each Pound of Flowers allow a-
bout one Pound of Loaf-Sugar,
and one Pint of White-Wine Vinegar, which boil to a Syrup, and
cover it ſcalding-hot. Thus you
may pickle* Clove-gillyflowers,
Elder, *and other Flowers, which
being eaten alone, make a very agreeable Salletine.*

14. Cucumbers. *Take the Gor-
kems, or ſmaller Cucumbers ;
put them into* Rape-Vinegar, *and
boyl, and cover them ſo cloſe, as
none of the Vapour may iſſue forth;
and also let them ſtand till the next
day : Then boil them in freſh
White-Wine Vinegar, with large
Mace, Nutmeg, Ginger, white
Pepper, and a little Salt, (according to diſcretion) ſtraining the
former Liquor from the Cucumbers ; and ſo place them in a Jarr,
or wide mouthed Glaſs, laying a*
lit-

little Dill and Fennel between each Rank ; and covering all with the fresh scalding-hot Pickle, keep all close, and repeat it daily, till you find them sufficiently green.

In the same sort Cucumbers of the largest size, being peel'd and cut into thin Slices, are very delicate.

Another.

Wiping them clean, put them in a very strong Brine of Water and Salt, to soak two or three Hours or longer, if you see Cause : Then range them in the Jarr or Barrellet with Herbs and Spice as usual ; and cover them with hot Liquor made of two parts Beer-Vinegar, and one of White-Wine Vinegar : Let all be very well closed. A Fortnight after scald the Pickle again, and repeat it, as above : Thus they will keep longer, and from being so soon

Appendix.

ſoon ſharp, eat crimp and well
taſted, tho' not altogether ſo green.
You may add a VValnut-Leaf,
Hyſop, Coſtmary, &c. and as
ſome do, ſtrow on them a little
Powder of Roch-Allom, which
makes them firm and eatable
within a Month or ſix VVeeks
after.

Mango of Cucumbers.

Take the biggeſt Cucumbers
(and moſt of the Mango ſize)
that look green : Open them on
the Top or Side; and ſcooping
out the Seeds, ſupply their Place
with a ſmall Clove of Garlick,
or ſome Roccombo Seeds. Then
put them into an Earthen Glazed
Jarr, or wide-mouth'd Glaſs, with
as much VVhite VVine Vinegar as
will cover them. Boil them in
the Vinegar with Pepper, Cloves,
Mace, &c. and when off the Fire,
as much Salt as will make a gentle
Brine;

Brine; and so pour all boyling-hot on the Cucumbers, covering them close till the next Day. Then put them with a little Dill, and Pickle into a large Skillet; and giving them a Boyl or two, return them into the Vessel again: And when all is cold, add a good Spoonful of the best Mustard, keeping it from the Air, and so have you an excellent Mango. VVhen you have occasion to take any out, make use of a Spoon, and not your Fingers.

Elder. See Buds.

Flowers. See Cowslips, and for other Flowers.

15. Limon. Take Slices of the thick Rind Limon, Boil and shift them in several VVaters, till they are pretty tender: Then drain and wipe them dry with a clean Cloth; and make a Pickle with a little VVhite-VVine Vinegar,

gar, one part to two of fair Water, and a little Sugar, carefully
scum'd. When all is cold, pour it
on the peel'd Rind, and cover it all
close in a convenient Glass Jarr.
Some make a Syrup of Vinegar, White-Wine and Sugar
not too thick, and pour it on
hot.

16. Melon. *The abortive and
after-Fruit of Melons being pickled
as* Cucumber, *make an excellent
Sallet.*

17. Mushrom. *Take a Quart
of the best White-Wine Vinegar;
as much of White-Wine, Cloves,
Mace, Nutmeg a pretty Quantity,
beaten together: Let the Spice boil
therein to the Consumption of half;
then taken off, and being cold pour the
Liquour on the* Mushroms; *but
leave out the boiled Spice, and cast
in of the same sort of Spice whole,
the Nutmeg only slit in Quarters,*

P   *with*

with some Limon-Peel, white Pepper; and if you please a whole raw Onion, which take out again when it begins to perish.

Another.

The Mushroms peel'd, &c. throw them into Water, and then into a Sauce-Pan, with some long Pepper, Cloves, Mace, a quarter'd Nutmeg, with an Onion, Shallot, or Roccombo-Seed, and a little Salt. Let them all boil a quarter of an hour on a very quick Fire: Then take out and cold, with a pretty Quantity of the former Spice, boil them in some White-Wine; which (being cold) cast upon the Mushroms, and fill up the Pot with the best White-Wine, a Bay-Leaf or two, and an Handful of Salt: Then cover them with the Liquour; and if for long keeping, pour Sallet-Oil over all, tho' they will be preserved a Year without it.

They

Appendix.

They are sometimes boil'd in Salt and Water, with some Milk, and laying them in the Colender to drain, till cold, and wiped dry, cast them into the Pickle with the White Wine, Vinegar and Salt, grated Nutmeg, Ginger bruised, Cloves, Mace, white Pepper and Limon Peel; pour the Liquor on them cold without boiling.

18. Nasturtium Indicum. Gather the Buds before they open to flower; lay them in the Shade three or four Hours, and putting them into an Earthen Glazed Vessel, pour good Vinegar on them, and cover it with a Board. Thus leting it stand for eight or ten Days: Then being taken out, and gently press'd, cast them into fresh Vinegar, and let them so remain as long as before. Repeat this a third time, and Barrel them up with Vinegar and a little Salt.

P 2   O-

Appendix.

Orange. *See* Limon.

20. **Potato.** *The small green Fruit (when about the size of the Wild Cherry) being pickled, is an agreeable Sallet. But the Root being roasted under the Embers, or otherwise, open'd with a Knife, the Pulp is butter'd in the Skin, of which it will take up a good Quantity, and is seasoned with a little Salt and Pepper. Some eat them with Sugar together in the Skin, which has a pleasant Crimpness. They are also stew'd and bak'd in Pyes, &c.*

21. **Purselan.** *Lay the Stalks in an Earthen Pan; then cover them with Beer-Vinegar and Water, keeping them down with a competent Weight to imbibe, three Days: Being taken out, put them into a Pot with as much White-Wine Vinegar as will cover them again; and close the Lid with Paste to keep in the Steam:*

Appendix.

Steam : Then set them on the Fire for three or four Hours , often shaking and stirring them : Then open the Cover, and turn and remove those Stalks which lie at the Bottom, to the Top, and boil them as before, till they are all of a Colour. When all is cold, pot them with fresh White-Wine Vinegar, and so you may preserve them the whole Year round.

22 Radish. *The Seed-Pods of this Root being pickl'd, are a pretty Sallet.*

23. Sampier. *Let it be gathered about* Michaelmas (*or the Spring*) *and put two or three Hours into a Brine of Water and Salt ; then into a clean Tin'd Brass Pot, with three parts of strong White-Wine Vinegar, and one part of Water and Salt, or as much as will cover the* Sampier, *keeping the Vapour from issuing out, by pasting down*

P 3 *the*

the Pot-lid, and so hang it over the Fire for half an Hour only. Being taken off, let it remain cover'd till it be cold; and then put it up into small Barrels or Jars, with the Liquor, and some fresh Vinegar, Water and Salt; and thus it will keep very green. If you be near the Sea, that Water will supply the place of Brine. This is the Dover Receit.

24. Walnuts. Gather the Nuts young, before they begin to harden, but not before the Kernel is pretty white: Steep them in as much Water as will more then cover them. Then set them on the Fire, and when the VVater boils, and grows black, pour it off, and supply it with fresh, boiling it as before, and continuing to shift it till it become clear, and the Nuts pretty tender: Then let them be put into clean Spring-VVater for two Days, changing it as before,
                                    with

Appendix.

with fresh, two or three times within this space: Then lay them to
drain, and dry on a clean course
Cloth, and put them up in a Glass
Jar, with a few Walnut Leaves,
Dill, Cloves, Pepper, whole Mace
and Salt; strowing them under
every Layer of Nuts, till the Vessel be three quarters full; and lastly, replenishing it with the best Vinegar, keep it well covered; and
so they will be fit to spend within three Months.

To make a *Mango* with them.

The Green Nuts prepared as before, cover the Bottom of the Jar
with some Dill, an Handful of
Bay-Salt, &c. and then a Bed of
Nuts; and so stratum upon stratum, as above, adding to the Spice
some Roccombo-Seeds; and fil-
ling the rest of the Jar with the
best White-Wine Vinegar, mingled with the best Mustard; and so

P 4   let

Appendix.

let them remain close covered, du-ring two or three Months time: And thus have you a more agreeable Mango *than what is brought us from abroad; which you may use in any Sauce, and is of it self a rich* Condiment.

Thus far Pickles.

25. Potage Maigre. *Take four Quarts of Spring-Water, two or three Onions stuck with some Cloves, two or three Slices of Limon-Peel, Salt, whole white Pepper, Mace, a Raze or two of Ginger, tied up in a fine Cloth (Lawn or Tiffany) and make all boil for half an Hour; Then having Spinage, Sorrel, white Beet-Chard, a little Cabbage, a few small Tops of Cives, wash'd and pick'd clean, shred them well, and cast them into the Liquor, with a Pint of blue Pease boil'd soft and strain'd, with a Bunch of sweet Herbs, the Top and Bottom of a* French Roll; *and so suffer it to boil during three Hours; and then*

dish

Appendix.

dish it with another small French Roll, and Slices about the Dish: Some cut Bread in slices, and frying them brown (being dried) put them into the Pottage just as it is going to be eaten.

The same Herbs, clean wash'd, broken and pulled asunder only, being put in a close cover'd Pipkin, without any other Water or Liquor, will stew in their own Juice and Moisture. Some add an whole Onion, which after a while should be taken out, remembring to season it with Salt and Spice, and serve it up with Bread and a Piece of fresh Butter.

26. Pudding of Carrot. Pare off some of the Crust of Manchet-Bread, and grate off half as much of the rest as there is of the Root, which must also be grated: Then take half a Pint of fresh Cream or New Milk, half a Pound of fresh Butter, six new laid Eggs (taking out three of the Whites)
mash

mash and mingle them well with the Cream and Butter: Then put in the grated Bread and Carrot, with near half a Pound of Sugar, and a little Salt; some grated Nutmeg and beaten Spice; and pour all into a convenient Dish or Pan, butter'd, to keep the Ingredients from sticking and burning; set it in a quick Oven for about an Hour, and so have you a Composition for any Root-Pudding.

27. Penny-royal. The Cream, Eggs, Spice, &c. as above, but not so much Sugar and Salt: Take a pretty Quantity of Peny-royal and Marigold Flower, &c. very well shred, and mingle with the Cream, Eggs, &c. four Spoonfuls of Sack; half a Pint more of Cream, and almost a Pound of Beef-Suet chopt very small, the Gratings of a Two-penny Loaf, and stirring all well together, put it into a Bag flower'd and tie it fast. It will be boil'd with-

within an Hour : Or may be baked in the Pan like the Carrot-Pudding. The sauce is for both, a little Rose-water, less Vinegar, with Butter beaten together and poured on it sweetned with the Sugar Caster.

Of this Plant discreetly dried, is made a most wholsom and excellent Tea.

28. Of Spinage. Take a sufficient Quantity of Spinach, stamp and strain out the Juice ; put to it grated Manchet, the Yolk of as many Eggs as in the former Composition of the Carrot-Pudding ; some Marrow shred small, Nutmeg, Sugar, some Corinths, (if you please) a few Carroways, Rose, or Orange-flower Water (as you best like) to make it grateful. Mingle all with a little boiled Cream ; and set the Dish or Pan in the Oven, with a Garnish of Puff-Paste. It will require but very moderate Baking. Thus have you Receits for Herb Puddings.

29.

Appendix.

29. Skirret-Milk *Is made by boiling the Roots tender, and the Pulp strained out, put into Cream or new Milk boiled, with three or four Yolks of Eggs, Sugar, large Mace and other Spice, &c. And thus is composed any other Root-Milk.* See Acetar. p. 65.

30. Tansie. *Take the Gratings or Slices of three Naples-Biscuits, put them into half a Pint of Cream, with twelve fresh Eggs, four of the Whites cast out, strain the rest, and break them with two Spoonfuls of Rose-water, a little Salt and Sugar, half a grated Nutmeg: And when ready for the Pan, put almost a Pint of the Juice of Spinach, Cleaver, Beets, Corn-Sallet, Green Corn, Violet, or Primrose tender Leaves, (for of any of these you may take your choice) with a very small Sprig of Tansie, and let it be fried so as to look green in the Dish.*

*Dish with a Strew of Sugar, and store
of the Juice of Orange : some affect to have it fryed a little brown
and crisp.*

31. Tart *of* Herbs. *An* Herb-
Tart *is made thus :* Boil fresh
Cream *or* Milk*, with a little grated* Bread *or* Naples-Biscuit *(which
is better) to thicken it ; a pretty
Quantity of* Chervile*,* Spinach*,*
Beete *(or what other Herb you
please) being first par-boil'd and
chop'd. Then add* Macaron*, or*
Almonds *beaten to a Paste, a little
sweet Butter, the* Yolk *of five*
Eggs*, three of the Whites rejected. To these some add* Corinths
*plump'd in Milk, or boil'd therein,
Sugar, Spice at Discretion, and
stirring it all together over the Fire,
bake it in the Tart-Pan.*

32. Thistle. *Take the long Stalks
of the middle Leaf of the* Milky-
Thistle*, about* May*, when they
are*

are young and tender : wash and scrape them , and boil them in Water, with a little Salt, till they are very soft, and so let them lie to drain. They are eaten with fresh Butter melted not too thin, and is a delicate and wholsome Dish. Other Stalks of the same kind may so be treated, as the Bur, being tender and disarmed of its Prickles, &c.

33. Trufles, *and other* Tubers, *and* Boleti, *are roasted whole in the Embers ; then slic'd and stew'd in strong Broth with Spice,* &c. *as* Mushroms *are.* Vide Acetar. p. 42.

34. Turnep. *Take their Stalks (when they begin to run up to seed) as far as they will easily break downwards : Peel and tie them in Bundles. Then boiling them as they do* Sparagus, *are to be eaten with melted Butter.* Lastly,

35.

Appendix.

35. Minc'd, *or* Sallet-all *forts.*

Take *Almonds* blanch'd in cold *Water*, cut them round and thin, and so leave them in the *Water*; Then have pickl'd *Cucumbers*, O-lives, *Cornelians, Capers, Berber-ries, Red-Beet,* Buds of Naſturti-um, *Broom,* &c. *Purſlan ſtalk, Sampier, Aſh-Keys, Walnuts, Muſhrooms* (and almoſt of all the pickl'd *Furniture*) with *Raiſins* of the *Sun ſton'd, Citron* and *Orange-Peel, Corinths* (well cleanſed and dried) &c. mince them ſeverally (except the *Corinths*) or all toge-ther; and ſtrew them over with any *Candy'd Flowers,* and ſo diſ-poſe of them in the ſame *Diſh* both mixt, and by themſelves. To theſe add roaſted *Maroons,* Piſtachios, Pine-Kernels, *and of Almonds* four times as much as of the reſt, with ſome *Roſe-water.* Here alſo come in the Pickled

Flow-

Appendix.

Flowers and Vinegar in little China Dishes. And thus have you an Universal Winter-Sallet, or an All *sort in Compendium, fitted for a City Feast, and distinguished from the* Grand-Sallet : *which show'd consist of the Green blanch'd and unpickled, under a stately* Pennash *of* Sellery, *adorn'd with Buds and Flowers.*

And thus have we presented you a Taste of our English Garden Housewifry *in the matter of* Sallets : *And though some of them may be* Vulgar, (*as are most of the best things*;) *Yet she was willing to impart them, to shew the Plenty, Riches and Variety of the* Sallet-Garden : *And to justifie what has been asserted of the Possibility of living* (*not unhapily*) *on* Herbs *and* Plants, *according to* Original *and* Divine Institution, *improved by* Time *and long Experience. And if we have admitted*

Mush-

Appendix.

Mushroms *among the rest (contrary to our Intention, and for Reasons given,* Acet. p. 43.) *since many will by no means abandon them, we have endeavoured to preserve them from those pernicious Effects which are attributed to, and really in them : We cannot tell indeed whether they were so treated and accommodated for the most Luxurious of the* Cæsarean Tables, *when that Monarchy was in its highest Strain of* Epicurism, *and ingross'd this* Haugout *for their second Course ; whilst this we know, that 'tis but what* Nature *affords all her Vagabonds under every Hedge.*

And now, that our Sallets *may not want a Glass of generous Wine of the same Growth with the rest of the Garden to recommend it, let us have your Opinion of the following.*

Cowslip-Wine. *To every Gallon of Water put two Pounds of Sugar ; boil it an Hour, and set it to cool : Then spread a good brown* Toast *on both Sides with* Yeast :

R   But

Appendix.

But before you make use of it, beat some Syrop of Citron *with it, an Ounce and half of Syrup to each Gallon of Liquor: Then put in the* Toast *whilst hot, to assist its Fermentation, which will cease in two* Days; *during which time cast in the* Cowslip-Flowers *(a little bruised, but not much stamp'd) to the Quantity of half a Bushel to two Gallons (or rather three Pecks) four* Limons *slic'd, with the Rinds and all. Lastly, one Pottle of White or Rhenish* Wine; *and then after two Days, tun it up in a sweet Cask. Some leave out all the Syrup.*

And here, before we conclude, since there is nothing of more constant Use than good Vinegar; *or that has so near an Affinity to all our* Acetaria, *we think it not amiss to add the following (much approved) Receit.*

Vinegar. *To every Gallon of Spring Water let there be allowed three Pounds of* Malaga-Raisins: *Put them in an Earthen Jarr, and place them where thay may have the*

hot-

Appendix.

hottest Sun, from May *till* Michaelmas : *Then pressing them well,* Tun *the Liquor up in a very strong* Iron-Hoop'd Vessel *to prevent its bursting. It will appear very thick and muddy when newly press'd, but will refine in the Vessel, and be as clear as Wine. Thus let it remain untouched for three Months, before it be drawn off, and it will prove* Excellent *Vinegar.*

Butter. Butter *being likewise so frequent and necessary an Ingredient to divers of the foregoing* Appendants : *It should be carefully melted, that it turn not to an Oil; which is prevented by melting it leisurely, with a little fair Water at the Bottom of the Dish or Pan; and by continual shaking and stirring, kept from boiling or over-heating, which makes it rank.*

Other rare and exquisite Liquors *and* Teas (Products *of our* Gardens *only*) *we might superadd, which we leave to our* Lady Housewives, *whose Province indeed all this while it is.* R 2 THE

THE
TABLE.

The TABLE.

Cau-

The TABLE.

The TABLE.

The TABLE.

The TABLE.

The TABLE.

The TABLE.

The TABLE.

The TABLE.

The TABLE.

The TABLE.

The TABLE.

APPENDIX.

Containing Receits for the Pickling, and other
ways of accommodating Winter-Sallets.

Artichoks.
Ashen-keys.
Asparagus.
Beans.
Beet.
Broom-Buds.
Carrot.
Champignons.
Chessnuts.
Cauly-flowers.
Cowslips.
Cucumber.
Elder-flowers.
Gilliflowers.
Herbs.
Limons.
Melon.

Mushrom.
Mustard.
Nasturtium.
Orange.
Parsnip.
Peny-royal.
Potato.
Purselan.
Radish.
Sampier.
Skirret.
Spinach.
Tansie.
Thistle. Turnip.
Vinegar. Walnuts.
Wine. Butter.

F I N I S.